Scale 1: 16 000 000; one inch to 250 miles. Conic Projection

Elevations and depressions are given in feet

Enchantment of the World

GREECE

By R. Conrad Stein

Consultants: Fotios K. Litsas, Ph.D., Classics Department, University of Illinois at Chicago, Chicago, Illinois; Ronald P. Legon, Ph.D., Professor of History, Acting Vice Chancellor for Research, Acting Dean of the Graduate College, University of Illinois at Chicago, Chicago, Illinois

Consultant for Reading: Robert L. Hillerich, Ph.D., Bowling Green State University, Bowling Green, Ohio

CHILDRENS PRESS ®
CHICAGO

The island of Thíra is a partially submerged volcanic crater.

Library of Congress Cataloging-in-Publication Data

Stein, R. Conrad.
  Greece.

  (Enchantment of the world)
  Includes index.
  Summary: Describes the geography, history, government,
culture, and people of Greece.
  1. Greece—Juvenile literature. [1. Greece]
I. Title. II. Series.
DF717.S72 1987   949.5   87-13225
ISBN 0-516-02759-X

Childrens Press, Chicago
Copyright ©1987 by Regensteiner Publishing Enterprises, Inc.
All rights reserved. Published simultaneously in Canada.
Printed in the United States of America.
1 2 3 4 5 6 7 8 9 10 R 96 95 94 93 92 91 90 89 88 87

Picture Acknowledgments
© **H. Armstrong Roberts/Camerique Stock Photography:**
4, 10, 29, 100 (right), 111
© **H. Armstrong Roberts:** Cover
Valan Photos: © Clara Parsons: 5; © Kennon Cooke: 19, 32
(left), 58, 86 (right); © Aubrey Diem: 76 (left), 90 (bottom
right), 92, 95 (left); © D. A. Farquhar: 80
Nawrocki Stock Photos: © Steve Vidler: 6, 93, 94, 102
(right); © Alx Phillips; 16 (top center), 97 (left); © Rui
Countinho: 70 (top left), 77 (left), 109 (top); © Peter
Panayiotou: 72, 107 (right); © Ted Cordingley: 79 (left)
© **Bob & Ira Spring:** 8, 110 (2 photos)
© **Roloc Color Slides:** 11 (left), 106 (right)

© **Jerome Wyckoff:** 11 (right), 79 (right), 90 (top), 98
The Photo Source © Colour Library International: 13, 25
(right), 45, 75 (left), 103 (top)
Root Resources: © Russel A. Kriete: 15, 74, 77 (right), 84
(right), 95 (right); © Leonard Gordon: 16 (bottom left), 101
(3 photos); © Jane H. Kriete: 32 (right); © Irene E. Hubbell:
75 (right); © Grete Schiodt: 107 (left), 109 (left center)
Third Coast: © John Nienhuis: 16 (top left), 20 (right);
© Phil Krejcarek: 25 (left), 31, 104; © Paul H. Henning: 26,
105 (bottom); © Michael A. Pawlowski: 54, 78, 84 (left)
Gartman Agency: © Arnold H. Crane: 16 (top right and
bottom center); © Christy Volpe: 33 (left), 96 (right), 108
(right), 109 (bottom right)
© **Mary Ann Brockman:** 16 (bottom right), 21, 23, 47 (left),
53, 88, 99 (2 photos), 108 (left)
Journalism Services: © Timmermann-Pictures: 20 left, 83
(left), 86 (bottom left), 103 (bottom); © Mark Snyder: 86
(top left), 102 (left)
© **Virginia Grimes:** 33 (right), 106 (left)
Historical Pictures Service, Chicago: 34 (left), 38
(2 photos), 40 (3 photos), 41 (left), 50 (left), 61 (2 photos),
63
© **Robert Frerck, Odyssey Productions:** 34 (right), 41
(center and right), 44, 47 (center and right), 50 (right), 70
(bottom), 83 (right), 97 (right), 105 (top), 109 (top)
The Metropolitan Museum of Art: 56
UPI: 64, 65 (2 photos), 68 (2 photos), 76 (right)
© **R. Conrad Stein:** 27, 70 (top right)
© **R/C Agency, Richard L. Capps:** 109 (bottom left)
Len W. Meents: Maps on pages 90, 92, 96, 100, 103
**Courtesy Flag Research Center, Winchester,
Massachusetts 01890:** Flag on back cover
Cover: A view of the Acropolis, Athens

Two Mikonos citizens

TABLE OF CONTENTS

The Acropolis dominates the skyline of Athens

Chapter 1

A MODERN STATE, AN ANCIENT LAND

In the center of Athens, the capital city of Greece, rises a famous flat-topped hill called the Acropolis. At its peak stand the ruins of a wondrous civilization. Prominent among them is the Parthenon, a temple built to honor the ancient gods. Next to the Pyramids of Egypt, the Parthenon is probably the world's most famous man-made structure.

Each day, hundreds of tourists from around the world stream up footpaths to visit the Parthenon and the surrounding buildings. Most feel shivers of awe as they gaze upon the stone monuments built by the people of Greece more than two thousand years ago. The Acropolis was the center of a culture where arts and sciences flourished, where philosophy reached its heights, and where democracy was born.

From the top of the Acropolis visitors also look down upon a sprawling city of glass and concrete. More than three million people rush to and from their jobs, seemingly unaware that they

A Corinthian colonnade stands in the ruins of the temple of Olympian Zeus, as seen from the Acropolis.

live in the shadow of what was perhaps history's greatest society. But the Greek people are proud of their past, and if they hurry by classical monuments without a second look, it is because they are pressured by the demands of modern life. Greece is a nation with one foot in the ancient world and the other in the twentieth century. The contrast between the past and the present and the people's hopes for the future makes Greece a fascinating land to discover.

Chapter 2

THE LAND

In the countryside, away from smog-filled Athens, the air above Greece is so pure it seems that wildflowers dazzle and the sea sparkles with greater fire than anywhere else on earth. But while this clear land delights the eyes, it leaves the belly rumbling. Much of the soil is a dismal blend of sand and pebbles, and rainfall is scant. Even in ancient times, when the population was a fraction of what it is today, the farmers of Greece were unable to feed all the people. The land of Greece merges stunning beauty with disappointing harshness. This marriage has molded the Greek soul.

GEOGRAPHY

Greece is the southernmost country in Europe. Its mainland bulges into the Mediterranean like a wedge. To the north, Greece shares a common border with Albania, Yugoslavia, and Bulgaria. The country is bordered on the east by Turkey. The sea accounts for the remainder of Greece's borders.

Greece's land area covers 50,944 square miles (131,944 square kilometers). The greatest distances on its mainland are: from north to south, 365 miles (587 kilometers), and from east to west, 345 miles (555 kilometers).

Fishermen's boats in a bay of Míkonos on the Aegean Sea

Nowhere in the country is one more than 85 miles (137 kilometers) from a seacoast. The Ionian Sea spreads to the west and the Aegean washes Greece's eastern shores. Though Greece is about the size of the state of Florida, it has more miles of coastline than the entire United States, excluding Alaska and Hawaii.

The nation's territory includes 437 islands, which are scattered about its adjacent seas. Many of the islands are rocky and treeless. Only 216 of them are inhabited. Some of the islands harbor a quaint way of life that makes them a haven for artists and writers. The largest of the Greek islands is Crete, a land steeped in history.

TOPOGRAPHY

The face of Greece is pitted with enormous wrinkles. On the mainland and many of the larger islands, mountain ranges follow each other like waves in the ocean. Mountains cover four-fifths of Greece and divide the country into valleys and plains.

Mount Olympus (left), in the north, is the highest point in Greece. The Pindus range (right) runs north to south near the center of the mainland.

The tallest mountain is snow-covered Mount Olympus, which is located in the north. Towering 9,570 feet (2,917 meters) into the sky, the mountaintop was once believed to be the home of the gods. From Olympus's lofty peak, Zeus, the father of the gods, was said to peer into every corner of the country with his all-seeing eyes.

The Pindus mountain range towers 8,000 feet (2,438 meters) along the Greek mainland, and the Taygetus rise to the south in the area called the Peloponnesus.

THE MAINLAND

The country's mainland can be divided into three sections: northern Greece, central Greece, and the Peloponnesus.

Northern Greece is made up of (running east to west) the regions of Thrace, Macedonia, and Epirus. Thrace and Macedonia are mountainous in the north, but are gifted with broad flat plains. Plains (flatlands) are unusual in Greece, and they are highly prized as farmland. Epirus, which lies in the northwest, has no significant plains.

Central Greece includes the region called Thessaly and the large island of Euboea, which hugs the east coast. Thessaly boasts three large plains where wheat is grown and stock pastured.

In the southeast, the mainland ends in a broad peninsula known as Attica, cut off from central Greece by mountains, and jutting out into the Aegean Sea. At the southern limit of the Attica plain, a few miles from the sea, stands Athens, the most important city of Greece.

The Peloponnesus is a landmass that, at first glance at a map, looks like an island lying close to the tip of the mainland's wedge. In fact, the name "Peloponnesus" means the Island of Pelops. A narrow land bridge, or isthmus, connects the Peloponnesus to the mainland.

THE ISLANDS

The islands that dot Greece's seas make up about 20 percent of the nation's territory. The islands can be grouped into two categories: The Ionian Islands in the Ionian Sea, west of the mainland, and the Aegean Islands in the Aegean Sea to the east.

A prevailing breeze blows across the Mediterranean from the west to the east, bringing rainfall to the Ionian Islands. Consequently the Ionians are lush, green, and lovely to look at from shipboard. Farmers there grow olives, grapes, and grains.

The Aegean Islands are less fortunate than those in the Ionian Sea. By the time the west to east breezes reach the Aegean, their moisture has already rained down on the Ionian Islands or the western mainland. Due to scant rainfall, soil on the Aegean

Windmills, used for irrigation in Crete

Islands yields crops grudgingly. Major Aegean Islands such as
Chios, Lesbos, Kós, Rhodes, and Sámos lie just a few miles off the
coast of Turkey.

Crete is the largest of all Greek islands, and supports a
population of more than half a million people. It is a greener land
than the Aegean Islands, but still suffers from insufficient rainfall.
Farmers on the Crete plains use windmills to pump underground
water and irrigate their fields. The whirling giants stand in
endless rows along the flatlands. Crete gave birth to the first
important European civilization about 5,000 years ago.

CLIMATE

Athens can become sweltering in the summer, while in the winter one needs a heavy jacket or a trenchcoat. Even in the winter, however, the city has a tropical feeling about it. In the midst of February, oranges grow on trees that stand in the city parks and line the boulevards. The average January temperature in the Greek capital is a little above freezing. During the summer, temperatures soar and sometimes break 100 degrees Fahrenheit (37.8 degrees Celsius).

Northern Greece, especially the mountainous regions of Thrace and Macedonia, has a temperate climate. The weather there is similar to that of central Europe. Winters can be harsh, and summers are cooler than those in Athens. Hardy pine trees grow in the north and in mountains everywhere, while palms, the symbol of the tropics, stand in the southern regions.

Altitude has a profound impact upon climate throughout Greece. Athens, which lies at about sea level, has significant snowfall only once every ten or fifteen years. The spring of 1987 was an exception, when an overnight snowfall buried the city. But the mountains surrounding the city are blanketed by snow at least once or twice a year.

Insufficient rainfall leaves Greece with no major rivers or lakes. In the summer, when many rivers dry to dust for lack of rain, villagers get their drinking water from underground wells.

FARMLAND

A Greek folktale says God made the countries surrounding Greece by sifting the earth through a strainer. When he finished

Olive groves on Crete, the largest of the Greek islands

creating those countries God dumped all the rocks and stones remaining in the strainer into the sea, and this waste material became Greece. The story is an exaggeration, for productive farmland does exist in Greece. Still, the tale is understandable because it was probably made up by a farmer who became frustrated while trying to grow wheat in rocks.

Only about 30 percent of the total land area of Greece can support crops. Most farms are small, averaging about 8 acres (3.2 hectares) in size. Still, these tiny farms nourish the Greek personality. It requires enormous genius and energy to grow a few bushels of olives, grapes, or vegetables from these patches of ground. And no matter how disappointing their yields are, Greek farmers gather in village coffeehouses in the evening to joke, laugh, and play cards. The practice of drowning one's troubles in smiles comes after centuries of eking out a living from a selfish but lovely land.

A variety of Greek faces, including a monk (top center) and a soldier (bottom right)

Chapter 3

THE PEOPLE

"What a strange machine man is. You put in bread, radishes and wine, and out come laughter, sighs and dreams."—Nikos Kazantzakis, a modern Greek writer.

WHO ARE THE GREEKS?

Greeks are a handsome people and usually have lean, athletic bodies. Often they have dark hair and dark complexions, and they tend to be shorter than northern Europeans. But there are loads of exceptions to this general description. Plenty of Greeks have blond or reddish hair, fair skin, and are tall enough to play basketball at an international level.

Ethnic minority groups such as Turks, Albanians, Gypsies, and Jews have lived in Greece for generations. The government considers them to be citizens, but since they prefer their own languages and religions they are regarded as outsiders by the majority of Greeks. Nevertheless, ethnic minorities live in harmony with their Greek neighbors.

POPULATION AND POPULATION DISTRIBUTION

The estimated 1986 population of Greece was over ten million people. Starting in the late 1950s, life in Greece changed dramatically when thousands of rural people flocked to the cities. Most of the country dwellers settled in Athens. Today greater Athens contains more than 30 percent of the nation's population. In 1920, only 6 percent of Greece's people lived in the Athens area. Since Athens is hemmed in by mountains, housing had to be built up instead of out. As a result, modern Athens has row after row of high-rise buildings towering over streets that swarm with traffic.

Piraeus, the port of Athens, is the third-largest city. Thessaloníki, in the Macedonian region, is second, and ranking fourth is Patras in the Peloponnesus. These cities also experienced a population explosion after World War II. The reason for the migration to the cities is simple. Jobs in urban areas offer three times better wages than comparative jobs in the country.

"Poverty and Greece are sisters," says an old Greek proverb. Most Greek farmland is stubbornly unproductive, and the nation has few natural resources. Since ancient times Greeks have sailed away to foreign lands to make a living. There was massive Greek immigration in the early twentieth century. The United States, Canada, and Australia all have large communities of people of Greek origin. Since Greeks are hardworking and thrifty, they are generally successful wherever they settle.

FAMILY LIFE

The family is the center of Greek society. Because Greeks are immensely friendly, outsiders are often invited to join their family

A family gathering

circle; but the outsider should remember that the Greek considers an injury or insult to one family member to be an injury to all. The Greek family practices some time-honored customs that seem strange to Americans and most other Europeans. The customs are changing because city life tends to break down old patterns, but some traditions are still revered.

When a Greek woman gets married, it is customary for her family to send her off with a certain sum of money or a piece of property to help her and her husband establish a new life. In old England such a treasure was called a dowry; in Greece it is referred to as a *proika*. Proikas granted by rich families can include an apartment building in Athens, stock in a bank, or a half interest in an oceangoing freighter. Poor families might provide a tiny farm or enough money to allow the son-in-law to attend a year or two of school. In either case the proika is intended as an aid to build the couple's future and should not be thought of as a frivolous gift.

These older Greek women (left) follow tradition, but the younger ones (right) may not.

Greek feminists object to the tradition of proikas. They say it puts a price on the woman's head and thus equates her with a cow or a horse. Largely because of feminist urging, the old laws that govern proikas were rescinded in the early 1980s. Meanwhile, the custom continues. Note this advertisement in a recent Athens newspaper: "Sturdy woman, capable of manual work, with proika of 100 olive trees and 25 acres, seeks a worthy husband."

A traditional Greek wedding ceremony is a marvelous contrast between the solemn and the outrageous. It begins in church with the bridegroom's godfather ceremoniously placing flower wreaths on the couple's heads. The wreaths, blessed by a priest, are linked with a ribbon. The guests watch this act in almost tomblike silence. But the celebration after the church service is an explosion of laughter, music, and dance. All guests are *required* to gorge themselves on food. The wild, unbridled fun a guest has at a Greek wedding remains etched in his or her memory forever.

A child enjoying an outing with his grandfather

In modern Athens very few married women hold jobs outside the home. The woman is expected to rear children, keep the apartment spotless, and prepare whatever dish her husband relishes. Certainly this pattern is changing, because a bright young woman can now get a university education or a job paying a decent wage. Still, old habits die hard. Most Greek men, and a sizable number of women, agree with a line stated in an ancient Greek play: "A woman should be everything inside the house and nothing outside it."

The Greek word *philotimo* describes a feeling of self-esteem that governs day-to-day behavior. The philotimo creed requires that a male never lose face in public. The emotions surrounding philotimo have a powerful influence on family life. A young boy grows up with the message that it is vital to always defend and never disgrace family honor.

Generally, both the Greek mother and father are lenient toward their children, but little boys are given special pampering. An American writer who lived many years in Athens told this story: "In a park one day [I saw] a three-year-old boy throw a stone at his sister with his parents looking on. His father reproved him with a single whack on the bottom. It was more than the child could stand. He clung, screaming and bawling, to his father's knees. The father relented immediately. He picked up the boy and kissed him on the eyes until joy shone through the boy's tears. Then he swung the child on his shoulders. Toying with his father's ears, the child continued to ride through the park on his moving throne of privilege, respectfully followed by his mother, and his tearful sister, who was told to stop whimpering."

SOCIAL LIFE

The Greeks have a hunger to communicate. Getting together with friends to chat pleasantly, argue, laugh, and gossip commands their social lives. The village square is a gathering spot for families. Boys and girls scamper about kicking a soccer ball while their parents sit on benches and chatter. Late at night it is common for someone to produce an accordion, and a group of friends bursts into song.

For the price of a cup of strong Turkish-blend coffee or a glass of wine, a man can sit at a *kafeneion* (coffeehouse) all night. The kafeneion, too, is a center of communication. Through the evening men shout and pound the tables while arguing politics, sports, or poetry. Those who are not arguing absorb themselves in games of cards, backgammon, or dominoes. In the 1980s (because of the demands of young men, but much to the horror of the older

Men outside a coffeehouse on the island of Hydra

customers) video games were introduced to the Greek
coffeehouses.

A woman may enter a kafeneion if she is accompanied by a
man. No law prevents a woman from coming into these
establishments alone or with a female companion, but it simply is
not done.

A Sunday outing usually means joining a crowd, and the
Greeks do this out of choice. The Greek fears solitude and does not
consider a holiday to be a chance to "get away from it all." Instead
a city family will leave Athens, park the car at the seashore, and
then seek the most crowded beach to spread their blanket. The
word for "private" in the Greek language is *idiotikos*, the root
word for "idiot."

Dating among young people is usually a group practice, too.
Boys and girls gather in gangs of fives and tens to go to the
zacharoplasteion (pastry shop), where they fill up on malts, ice-
cream concoctions, or sinfully rich Greek pastry. Certainly a boy
and girl will go out alone together but, like so much of life in
Greece, dating patterns have changed in the 1970s and 1980s. Not

long ago a teenage couple going out to the movies would need a chaperone, usually an older brother or an uncle, to accompany them. A chaperone is no longer required, but shadows of family honor and the philotimo code loom over the couple, demanding proper behavior.

Adults who go out with friends at night often celebrate into the very wee hours. Many businesses shut down at 1:30 P.M. to allow their employees to go home, enjoy a large lunch, and take a short nap before coming back to work at about five o'clock. Armed with this midafternoon nap, a Greek worker can afford to stay up late. Service at many restaurants begins at 9:00 P.M., and dinners can be ordered well after midnight. The last feature at a movie theater starts at about two in the morning. However, the pressures of a modern economy are changing Greek nightlife. Large factories have abandoned the afternoon nap custom and adopted nine-to-five hours.

Finally, from the point of view of an outsider, Greek social life is highlighted by an amazing acceptance of strangers. A chance conversation on the street between a factory worker and a foreigner can easily lead to the foreigner being invited to the family dinner. No one can explain the reason for this remarkable cordiality, but visitors to the country have hailed it through the ages. The Greek language is perhaps the only one in the world where the word for "stranger," *xenos*, is the same as the word for "guest."

RELIGION

At least 95 percent of all Greeks claim membership in the Greek Orthodox church, a part of the Eastern Orthodox church. Until

The interior and exterior of Greek Orthodox churches

1054, the Eastern Orthodox and Roman Catholic churches were one body. Theological, political, and cultural differences split the church in two, and those differences were never completely reconciled.

Religious beliefs influence the lives of practically every Greek. Villagers ask a priest to sprinkle holy water on their land before spring planting. In the cities a special service is conducted at construction sites before workers begin erecting new buildings. All Greek ships at sea have a pictorial representation of St. Nicholas, the patron saint of sailors, somewhere aboard the vessel.

Despite the power religion holds over everyday life, Greeks are not devout churchgoers. Aside from the special Easter celebrations, services are attended mainly by old women and young children. And the Greeks often defy their church's teachings by clinging to old superstitions.

"Ye men of Athens, I perceive that in all things ye are too superstitious." St. Paul preached these words to the Greeks almost

A display of newspapers at a vendor's stand in Athens

two thousand years ago, but the people failed to heed his counsel. It is estimated that fifteen thousand fortune-tellers and professional astrologers operate in Greece. Witches (nonmedical doctors who cure by chants and charms) are still called upon by sick people. Some country villages reenact ancient springtime rituals and sacrifice animals. Trivial taboos abound: Don't leave a scissors open or people will talk behind your back. Allowing the closet door to stand ajar causes neighbors to gossip about the family. If you wash your hair on a Sunday, you are destined to have a blue Monday. The list goes on and on.

LANGUAGE

Greek is the oldest language spoken in Europe. If the philosopher Aristotle, who lived before the time of Christ, returned tomorrow, he could, with some difficulty, read the morning newspapers. However, the pronunciation of words and their structure is radically different today than in ancient times. Modern Greek incorporates Turkish, Slavic, Albanian, Italian, and French words.

The Greek language uses its own alphabet. Its letters are far different from those of the Latin alphabet, which are used in this

On a phone booth, both the English and Greek words for telephone are visible.

book. For example, the letter that carries the "s" sound (*sigma* in Greek) is the letter Σ in the Greek alphabet. The Greek alphabet has twenty-four letters to Latin's twenty-six. For the benefit of tourists, signs in Greek cities are posted in the Greek alphabet alongside another sign with the corresponding Greek word spelled out in the western alphabet.

English is the second language for most Greeks. Students begin studying English in grade school. Since English is the language of tourism and technology—two areas that produce jobs—young Greeks are driven to master it. University-educated Greeks speak English, French, and a smattering of German.

Lastly, Greek people use a colorful form of body language. Italians are famous for talking with their hands, but Greeks seem to communicate with their whole beings. A foreigner watching a group of men carry on what appears to be a heated discussion in a coffeehouse might wonder when the first punch will be thrown. But suddenly the foreigner is surprised to see the men engaging in warm hugs. They weren't arguing at all. They were merely expressing their eternal friendship.

Chapter 4

THE BEGINNINGS

"The gods did not reveal everything to men at the beginning, but men, as they seek in time, find something better."—Thales, the earliest known Greek philosopher.

LEGENDARY GREECE

Prometheus was a godlike figure who was kind to mortal men and women. He stole the secret of fire-making from the gods and gave it to the people of earth. The theft infuriated Zeus, the chief of the gods, and he sent an enchanting woman named Pandora to earth. When Pandora opened a sealed box she carried from the heavens, evils such as hunger, disease, and hard labor drifted out and forever plagued mankind. Only the feeling of hope remained in the box and therefore within the grasp of men and women.

In a story similar to that told in the Bible, Zeus decided to destroy humanity by means of a massive flood. Prometheus warned two mortals, Deucalion and his wife Pyrrha, about the coming floods and advised them to build a wooden ark. The couple floated in the ark for nine days before landing on a mountaintop as the only humans left on earth. They repopulated the world by casting stones. The stones thrown by Deucalion became men and the stones thrown by Pyrrha became women.

A favorite place to watch the sunset is at Cape Sounion on the Aegean Sea, where it is seen above through the ruins of the temple to Poseidon, the sea god.

Hundreds of myths (traditional stories often dealing with supernatural beings) told of a fabulous age when gods and goddesses and heroic figures walked the earth with ordinary men and women. These tales, referred to as Greek mythology, were passed on by generations of storytellers. The gods never died nor did they grow old. In the blink of an eye they could become a bull, a lion, or a soaring bird. Yet these lofty beings often behaved like spoiled children. They lived, cheated, bickered with each other, and flew into violent rages of jealousy at the slightest provocation. Greek myths also told of *heroes* who were godlike in their powers, but suffered old age and death.

The Greeks of historic times, including some of the greatest thinkers in history, believed this legendary age of gods and heroes really existed. In fact, the Greeks thought they were the descendants of the divinities of a bygone age.

For the most part, archaeologists give us less fanciful clues about life in Greece before recorded history. Sometimes, however, scientific evidence lends a curious confirmation to the legends of gods and heroes. Farming began on the mainland around 6000 B.C., and perhaps even earlier on the Aegean Islands. Eventually the primitive farmers established remarkable cultures.

THE MINOAN CIVILIZATION

"There is a land called Crete in the midst of the wine-dark sea, a fair land . . . and therein are many men innumerable in ninety cities . . . and among these cities is the mighty city Knossus, wherein Minos when he was nine years old began to rule, he who held converse with great Zeus."—from the *Odyssey* of Homer.

On the long narrow island of Crete, the first important civilization in Europe rose around the year 3000 B.C. It was called the Minoan Culture after King Minos who, tradition says, ruled the island. The Minoan people built imposing palaces and houses, some of which were five stories high—a tower in those days. A few of the buildings had toilets that flushed—this while most Europeans still lived in caves. The Minoans made jewelry, fashioned pottery with intricate designs, and developed a written language. Superb sailors, they traded goods in all parts of the Mediterranean world. The Minoans delighted in what had to be a very dangerous form of bullfighting. Pictures on vases show young men doing flying somersaults over the backs of charging bulls.

Archaeological excavations have uncovered a maze of corridors, rooms, and stairways that make up the palace at Knossus, built long before the time of Christ.

A Minoan story tells of a monster called the Minotaur that was half bull and half man. King Minos captured the Minotaur and imprisoned him in a maze of hallways known as a labyrinth. At regular intervals, King Minos sent young men and women into the labyrinth as a sacrifice for the Minotaur. The hero Theseus finally killed the Minotaur and found his way out of the labyrinth by following an unwound spool of thread that was given to him by Ariadne, King Minos' daughter.

When archaeologists excavated the palace at Knossus, they discovered ruins containing a confusing array of hallways. Some scholars have suggested the building was the labyrinth referred to in the ancient story. However, it must be pointed out, no bones of a creature even remotely resembling a Minotaur have been discovered anywhere on earth.

Beautiful artifacts can be seen in Crete, such as vases (left) in the Archaeological Museum and a fresco (right) entitled Ladies in Blue *at Knossus.*

The Minoan Culture ended with dramatic suddenness in the mid-1400s B.C. One theory explaining its sudden demise holds that a volcano exploded on the island of Thíra just 70 miles (113 kilometers) north of Crete, causing earthquakes that tore Minoan buildings to pieces, killed thousands of people, and ruined crops.

THE MYCENAEANS

Around 2000 B.C., Greek-speaking people built the palace of Mycenae in the Peloponnesian Peninsula. Its massive walls contained single stones, some of which weighed as much as 120 tons. Three such stones, crowned by an A-shaped structure composed of two lions, form the famous "Lion's Gate" entrance.

Mycenaean culture was, for the most part, the equal of the older Minoan civilization. These early Greek people were skilled metalworkers. Golden death masks and exquisite silver drinking cups have been discovered in their tombs and in the ruins of their cities. They used bronze to make swords, daggers, and shields. The

*The Lion's Gate of Mycenae (left)
and a gold death mask of Agamemnon (right),
who was king of Mycenae*

Mycenaeans preserved the art of writing. But while the Minoans preferred to live at peace with their neighbors, the Mycenaeans delighted in waging war. Their fleets of pirate ships ranged as far as Egypt and Asia Minor, and their marauding armies terrorized their neighbors.

THE TROJAN WAR

The long poem, the *Iliad*, tells us that a war between the Mycenaeans and the city of Troy began when a Trojan man named Paris ran off with lovely Helen, the wife of the Mycenaean king. When the Mycenaean Greeks discovered the abduction, a great army sailed to Troy. To this day, Helen of Troy is thought of as a woman of unmatched beauty, whose face "launched a thousand ships."

For ten years the Greeks lay siege to the walled city of Troy, but were unable to capture it. The *Iliad* says that during the siege Greek officers fought among themselves. Agamemnon, the king of Mycenae, insulted his bravest warrior, Achilles. In return, Achilles spent much of the siege brooding in his tent.

Schliemann excavated Troy (left) following the directions laid down in Homer's Iliad. *Right: a bust of Homer*

Adding intrigue to the conflict was the bizarre behavior of the gods. They viewed the siege from a high mountaintop and took a sporting interest in the outcome. Zeus favored Troy, but his wife Hera hoped the Greeks would win. So Hera lulled Zeus to sleep to prevent him from helping the Trojans. Apollo was associated with the sea and he sided with the Greeks, a seafaring people.

For 3,000 years after the Trojan War, people have looked upon the *Iliad* and its companion book, the *Odyssey*, as compelling works of fiction. Troy was thought of as a city that Homer, the author of the two books, imagined. Then, in 1870, the German-born archaeologist Heinrich Schliemann found the ruins of Troy on the coast of what is now Turkey. He discovered the ancient city by following the descriptions laid down in Homer's *Iliad*.

THE DORIAN INVASION

Late in the 1100s B.C., a warrior band called the Dorians swept over the Greek mainland and sailed to the islands. Although the Dorians lacked the Greeks' political organization and could not even read or write, their conquest of the land was almost complete. The Dorians possessed weapons made of a wondrous new substance—iron. In battle, their iron swords crushed the bronze shields used by Greek warriors. Centuries later, a Greek adage ran, "The discovery of iron had been to the hurt of man."

The Dorian conquest shrouded Greece in a dark age. Political order and public safety became dim memories. War flourished, robbers ruled the roadways, and poverty deepened and spread. Even the art of writing, once revered in Greece, was forgotten. Centuries passed before the people of Greece learned anew the value of the written word.

To escape their Dorian conquerors, many Greek people fled to the sea. Greek settlements appeared on the mainland of Italy, and in Sicily, southern France, northern Africa, and Spain. Marseilles, France, and Naples, Italy, developed as Greek towns. Naples comes from the Greek word *Neapolis*, meaning "New City."

In Italy, the people called the Greek settlements *Magna Graecia*. The name Greece eventually came from that term. The ancient Greeks referred to themselves as *Hellenes* and their homeland as *Hellas*. Their arts, folktales, and religious beliefs, which they spread throughout the Mediterranean, are referred to by historians as the *Hellenic culture*.

THE RISE OF THE CITY-STATES

Toward the end of the Dorian period, towns and their surrounding farms formed what were called *poleis*, or city-states. Because they were separated by rugged mountain chains, each city-state spoke its own dialect of the Greek language, minted its own coins, and drew its own laws.

The most important city-states early in Greek history were Athens and Thebes in central Greece, and Corinth and Sparta on the Peloponnesian Peninsula. The city of Argos, rising near the site of Mycenae, controlled the largest plain in the Peloponnesus. Wealth and military power allowed Argos to dominate her neighbors for centuries, until her power was destroyed by Sparta.

Corinth and Sparta were both Dorian settlements. Spartan society was devoted to war. Corinth was located at the narrow isthmus that connected the mainland with the Peloponnesus. A vital crossroads for trade, Corinth became a wealthy city.

The jewel of all city-states was Athens. With its port city of Piraeus on one side and the Attica plains on the other, it commanded both land and sea. Early in its history Athens was ruled by a king, and a group of aristocrats owned its most productive farmland. Their remarkable leaders, such as Solon, Pisistratus, and Cleisthenes set Athens on a new path between 600 and 500 B.C. Under their rule, a revolutionary type of government called democracy, or rule by the many, developed. The Athenians were the first people to practice democracy on a large scale.

WAR WITH PERSIA

King Darius of Persia longed to add Greece to his empire. In 490 B.C. the Athenians and their allies met the Persian army at the plain of Marathón. The Athenian forces were outnumbered two to one. Nevertheless, their army routed the Persians. The historian Herodotus, who lived during that time, claimed the battle cost Darius 6,400 soldiers while the Greeks lost only 192 men.

After the battle, the Greek commander sent his swiftest runner, Pheidippides, to Athens to carry the news. Pheidippides, who was already exhausted after running a message to Sparta and back, reached the city, gasped out the words, "Rejoice, we conquer," then fell dead. Today, the celebrated marathon race, the crowning event of the modern Olympic Games, covers a distance of 26 miles, 385 yards (42.2 kilometers) — the length of Pheidippides' run from Marathón to Athens.

Ten years after Marathón, King Xerxes, the son of Darius, marched toward Athens with a powerful army. At a valley called Thermopylae, he clashed with an advance guard that included only three hundred Spartans. The Spartans, schooled to be soldiers since boyhood, fought with a ferocity that astonished the Persians. Herodotus wrote, "They defended themselves to the last, such as still had swords using them, and the others resisting with their hands and teeth."

The heroic Spartan resistance gave the Athenians time to evacuate their city. When Xerxes entered Athens, he found little more than empty houses. In a fury he destroyed the temples and buildings on top of Athens' sacred hill, the Acropolis. He also slaughtered the few Athenians who remained in the city.

The Athenian navy still commanded the seas, and while Xerxes watched from water's edge, a titanic sea battle took place near Athens. In those days, warring ships attempted to ram each other. The Athenian ships, faster and more maneuverable, smashed into the Persians. Soon the sea was choked with the wreckage of Persian vessels and the bodies of their sailors. With his navy in shambles, Xerxes was eventually forced to withdraw.

The victory over the Persians was the ancient Greeks' finest hour. It demonstrated that the various city-states were invincible when they were able to put aside their differences. Also, this victory served as a harbinger of the glorious age to come.

A reconstruction (above)
of the original Acropolis
in Athens. The large
building on the right is
the Parthenon, much of which
is still standing today.
Left: A drawing of the interior
of the Parthenon as it once was.
The bronze statue of Athena
as a warrior was designed
by Phidias.

Chapter 5

ANCIENT GLORY

If ever a people changed the face of the world, it was the Greeks who lived three and four centuries before Christ. Without their brilliant society, the journey of mankind would have taken a different and more troublesome direction. "We are all Greeks," wrote the British poet Shelley in the early 1800s. "Our laws, our literature, our religion, our arts, have roots in Greece. But for Greece . . . we might still have been savages."

THE GOLDEN AGE

It is a bright summer morning in the year 438 B.C. The sun climbs over the mountains into the magically clear sky above Athens. The city buzzes with excitement because today Athenian officials will dedicate the newly completed Parthenon. Built to replace the temples destroyed by the Persians, it is the first and will be the finest of the new buildings atop the sacred Acropolis.

A parade of gray-haired priests, young men astride horses, and girls carrying olive branches winds up the main path to the hilltop. All of Athens—from the statesman to the beggar—line the road to watch. Although we do not know the details of the ceremonies, we do know some of the famous people who were alive and residing in the city at the time, so we can assume a role call of the luminaries.

Left to right: Socrates, Hippocrates, and Phidias

Hippocrates watches the parade flanked by half a dozen of his students. He is creating a revolution by taking medicine out of the shrouds of superstition and into the realm of science. Graduating medical students are still required to take his oath, which says, in part, "With purity and with holiness I will pass my life and practice my art." Standing near the doctor is a leading scientist named Anaxagoras. He recently stunned the Athenian community by declaring that the sun is not really a god at all. Instead, it is a huge burning rock.

Fanning himself with a leaf is the playwright Sophocles. Before his death, Sophocles will write more than one hundred plays, many of which are still performed. Like so many Greeks, he is a man of numerous dimensions, having served as a soldier, a priest, and a statesman of Athens. His rival playwright, Euripides, also watches the procession. Euripides' mind wrestles with thoughts that are both deeply religious and darkly cynical. One of his recent plays contains a line that shocks Greek conservatives: "Oh, Zeus, if there be a Zeus, for I know of him only by report . . ."

The procession passes a robed figure who, depending on his mood, is smiling or scowling at the crowd. He is the philosopher Socrates who teaches in the streets, the marketplace, or the goat fields. He burns with the need to question everything, believing

Left to right: Euripides, Pericles, and Sophocles

that ignorance—the lack of investigation—is the cause of all evil. He once said, "The unexamined life is not worth living." His most famous student, Plato, has yet to be born. Although Socrates is generally admired, his enemies have deemed him to be a dangerous influence on young minds.

At the peak of the Acropolis the aging architect and sculptor Phidias, who designed the Parthenon, gazes at his creation. The magnificent building stands sixty feet (eighteen meters) tall and is ringed by forty-six columns. The top outer wall contains a series of statues called *metopes*, which show scenes from the Trojan War and events dating back to the legendary age of myths when gods walked the earth with men and women. Inside, a statue of the goddess Athena stands so tall her head practically brushes the ceiling. Her robe, made of solid gold, is removable and serves as the city treasury.

On top of a speaker's platform stands Pericles, the uncrowned king of Athens. For more than twenty years he has been annually reelected as one of Athens' ten *strategoi* (generals). His long career and continuous popularity with the citizens gives him unprecedented influence over public affairs. Pericles' years of power have ever after been known as "the Golden Age of Greece."

The dedication of the Parthenon was the golden moment of a golden age. It is not known what Pericles said, but one of his speeches that was preserved by the historian Thucydides would have been appropriate for that glittering event: "Mighty indeed are the marks and monuments of our empire which we have left. Future ages will wonder at us as the present age wonders at us now."

LIFE DURING THE GOLDEN AGE

Scores of city-states dotted the map of Greece during the fifth century B.C. At the time, Athens and Sparta were the most important.

War and the preparation for war dominated the life of Sparta. The Spartans believed comforts and luxury soften men, so they stripped the frills from their everyday lives. Even during peacetime, men took their meals in a public dining hall with members of their army unit. The food was deliberately cooked to be tasteless, and the portions served were tiny. Today if one lives on meager meals and in harsh housing, he or she is said to be "living a Spartan existence."

At age eight, a Spartan boy left his family and was assigned to a regiment. There he learned wrestling, running, and knife fighting. Few schools taught reading. The strongest, most ferocious boy in the class was appointed group leader. He was allowed, and even encouraged, by the teachers, to beat other boys with a stick if their athletic skills failed to measure up to standards. A Spartan youth was expected to suffer these whippings without so much as a whimper. The boys were required to sleep outside during the winter. Exercises were conducted in the nude, so that no boy could hide a frail or a flabby body.

The warrior citizens of Sparta were outnumbered ten to one by their noncitizen subjects, called *helots* and *perioeci*. The helots worked the citizens' land, like serfs, and had no political rights. The perioeci were mostly craftsmen and merchants who governed their own small towns, paid taxes to the Spartans, and had no voice in the affairs of the city-state.

Strangely, Spartan women lived freer lives than women in other city-states. With the men preoccupied by either fighting wars or preparing for war, the women were left to run everyday activities. Women eventually built up great economic power. Aristotle claimed that women owned two-fifths of Spartan lands.

A boy's education in Athens was a world removed from the military society of Sparta. From ages seven to eighteen, boys attended school where they studied reading, poetry, music, and mathematics. Practically all teachers required the boys to memorize long chapters of the *Iliad* and the *Odyssey*. Discipline in class was strict. Protagoras, an Athenian professor who lived in the fifth century B.C., claimed, "If [the boy] obeys, well and good; if not, he is straightened by threats and blows with a piece of bent or warped wood."

Athens provided no formal schooling for girls. Girls were taught by their mothers and sisters to mend, sew, and make the family's clothing. Adult women in Athens could not vote and enjoyed little power in the city's economy. Yet the plays the Greek men so enjoyed, often had women exerting a strong influence on the story.

Slaves performed the city's chores. During the Golden Age, one out of every three people in Athens was a slave. Generally slaves

The Agora, the marketplace below the Acropolis

were treated well and could look forward to eventual freedom. A good number of teachers were educated slaves. Still, many Athenian intellectuals denounced the institution of slavery. The playwright Euripides wrote, "Slavery,/that thing of evil, by its nature evil,/Forcing submission from man to what/No man should yield to."

Social life in Athens centered on the Agora, or marketplace, which spread below the Acropolis. In it, small storekeepers sold olives, olive oil, almonds, bread, vegetables, and pottery. But the Agora was far more than just a place where people bought goods. A temple rose on the grounds and served as a center of worship. At a nearby athletic field, Athenians participated in foot races, wrestling, and discus throwing. The Agora was also the meeting place of philosophers and a schoolground for Athenian boys, since there were no formal classrooms.

Although life in Athens, Sparta, and the other city-states varied, two institutions, religion and athletics, united the Greek world.

All Greeks worshiped basically the same gods. Holy shrines called *oracles* were religious centers. It was believed that pilgrims

Olympia lies in a fertile valley.

who visited oracles were allowed to glimpse future events. The oracle at the city of Delphi was one of the most revered places in ancient Greece.

Once every four years, athletes, judges, and spectators came from even the remotest islands to the town of Olympia to participate in the Olympic Games. The Games were so important the Greek calendar was based on their beginnings and endings. To celebrate the Olympics, the Greeks called a temporary halt to any wars that might have been going on at the time. Even the war-loving state of Sparta complied with the ban. The Greeks of "primitive times" would have been outraged if wars, boycotts, political demonstrations, or terrorism marred their Games, as they have done so frequently in the twentieth century.

AN ETERNAL LEGACY

Greece's Golden Age is often called its Classical Period. Classical Greece gave future generations timeless gifts of art, literature, science, and philosophy.

Sculpture was the art form most favored by the Greeks of classical times. By the Classical Period, sculpture had reached its height of excellence. Famous sculptors of the fifth century B.C. included Myron, Phidias, and Polyclitus. These masters of stone carved idealized statues of well formed men and beautiful women, which testified to the Greek belief in the wonder of mankind. Later generations of sculptors imitated but never quite duplicated the achievement of Classical Greece.

The influence of Classical Greek architecture echoed for centuries. Three distinct styles of architecture—Doric, Ionic, and Corinthian—can be seen in the columns of Greek temples. The Doric column is the oldest and plainest style, using simple, geometric shapes. To symbolize strength, the Parthenon used Doric columns. The Ionic column is slender and graceful, crowned by a scroll-like capital (head of a pillar or column). Corinthian columns are even more ornamental with capitals imitating acanthus leaves. Greek architecture had such a profound impact on future generations that public buildings in Europe and America, built in the 1800s and early 1900s, were often designed after temples of Classical Greece.

During the Golden Age, philosophers were looked upon as a class of people similar to soldiers or storekeepers. The philosopher's job was to think, question, debate, and teach. In Athens' marketplace Socrates taught Plato, who in turn taught Aristotle. Their ideas are still studied by scholars.

*Columns of Classical Greek architecture are
(left to right) Doric, Ionic, and Corinthian.*

Socrates devoted his life to seeking the truth, but his
unorthodox views on religion and the role of authority won him
powerful enemies. Socrates was brought to trial, where he boldly
refused to recant his beliefs. The court sentenced him to death by
poison. In his book *Phaedo*, Plato gives a moving account of how
Socrates, surrounded by his disciples, drank the poison and
calmly waited for death. Today, Socrates is one of the most
admired figures in history. His life and death are a model of
nobility and courage, and he will always be hailed as a shining
star of the Golden Age of Greece.

GREEK AGAINST GREEK

It is a sad lesson in world history that golden ages are always
short, and they usually end in war. Such was the case in 431 B.C.,
when a war broke out between Athens and Sparta and raged for
the next twenty-eight years.

Athens, with its splendid navy, held sway at sea, but no city-state could hope to defeat the Spartan army on land. With Pericles in charge, Athens avoided a land battle. When Pericles died after a great plague swept Athens, his successors quarreled, leaving the city's leadership in a state of confusion. The Spartans persuaded their old enemies, the Persians, to loan them money to build a fleet. In a surprise attack, the Spartans destroyed the Athenian navy, bringing final victory in what historians call the Peloponnesian War.

Greek society was the ultimate loser, because the long and bloody Peloponnesian War weakened all the city-states. Meanwhile, the northern province of Macedonia grew steadily stronger. Under the leadership of Philip II, a brilliant general and crafty diplomat, Macedonia unified northern Greece and defeated the city-states at the battle of Chaeronea. A fiery figure in the Macedonian court was Alexander, the king's son. The pages of history called him Alexander the Great.

THE WORLD OF ALEXANDER

While growing up in Macedonia, Alexander enjoyed a Greek education. As a boy he memorized the entire *Iliad*. At thirteen he was taught by Aristotle and fell under that philosopher's spell. Alexander idolized Greek heroes of old and believed Hellenic culture to be superior to all others.

When he was twenty his father was murdered, leaving Alexander master of a small but powerful army. His first test came when the people of Thebes rebelled against Macedonian rule. Alexander stormed the city, crushed its army, and sold its three thousand citizens into slavery. As final punishment, he tore down every house in Thebes save one. He spared the house of the long-dead poet Pindar, who had praised the athletes of the Olympic Games.

Next, Alexander, uniting the Greeks, marched east toward Greece's ancient enemy, Persia. His allies numbered only thirty-five thousand men, and he was certain to meet forces at least twice that size. But Alexander possessed gifts denied most men. He was brilliant in maneuvering his infantry to strike enemy ranks at their weakest point. While leading cavalry charges, his bravery became a legend.

City after city fell before Alexander's onslaught. At Susa, he captured a king's treasury of gold and silver so vast one historian claimed it took twenty thousand mules and five thousand camels to remove it. Upon arriving in Gordium, Alexander was taken to see a famous rope tied in a mystical knot. Legends claimed that anyone who possessed the intelligence to untie the knot would rule all of Asia. Alexander looked at the knot, drew his sword, and cut the rope in half with one stroke.

When Alexander marched on Egypt he was welcomed as a god. He founded the city of Alexandria, which flourished as a center of culture and trade. He took the long, tortuous journey to the temple and the oracle of Zeus-Ammon. There, the priests proclaimed him a son of the gods, destined to command the world.

After conquering the entire Persian Empire, Alexander led his forces toward the Indus River, which, to the ancients, was the world's end. He fought an Indian army whose soldiers rode fearsome war elephants. The thundering beasts panicked Alexander's horses, but he won the battle by attacking from an unexpected quarter.

Although he knew only victory on the battlefield, Alexander was unable to defeat the inner demons that plagued him. In a

Left: A statue of Alexander the Great
Right: Hadrian's Gate in Athens, built in A.D. 132

drunken fury he killed his best friend Clitus. When his beloved horse Bucephalus was killed in battle, Alexander sank into a deep depression that lasted months. At the height of his powers he often sat alone brooding. Some historians suggest he cried because he knew of no more worlds to conquer.

In 323 B.C., Alexander the Great died of fever at age thirty-three. He had no heirs and the empire he carved out soon collapsed. But he will always be remembered as history's foremost military genius. More important, he brought Hellenic culture to the ends of the known world, and he encouraged a blending of politics, literature, religion, philosophy, and the arts. Historians call the rich mixture that emerged after Alexander's time the *Hellenistic Civilization*. As the Greek historian Plutarch said of Alexander, "He believed that he had a mission from God to bring men into harmony with each other and to reconcile the world."

Chapter 6

CAPTIVE GREECE

Greek language and culture survived and even flourished after the death of Alexander, but mainland Greece and its islands became yoked to a string of conquerors. The period of captivity lasted more than two thousand years. The first of its overlords was ever-expanding Rome which, after a series of battles, controlled all of Greece and Macedonia by the 140s B.C.

THE ROMAN PERIOD

"Captive Greece took Rome captive," wrote the Roman poet Horace. Unable to match the Greeks' achievements in the arts and sciences, the conquerors fashioned themselves after the conquered. Roman aristocrats sent their children to Greece to be taught by Hellenic scholars. Roman intellectuals studied Greek philosophy, poetry, and ways of thinking.

Hadrian, the Roman emperor who reigned in the second century A.D., considered Greece to be his spiritual home. He lived in Athens from A.D. 120 to 128. He befriended the Greek historian Plutarch, founded a library, and built an archway called "Hadrian's Gate," which still stands in front of a park in central Athens.

The Christian apostle St. Paul was an important visitor to Greece during the Roman period. He established a Christian community at Corinth in A.D. 51, and visited Athens. Although Jesus Christ spoke to his followers in the Aramaic tongue, his apostles (including St. Paul) wrote their Gospels in Greek. At the time, Greek was widespread because Alexander the Great had brought it east while the Romans carried the language to the west. So the ancient language of the Greeks served to proclaim the new religion of Christ, which quickly changed the character of the world.

Politically and economically, Greece suffered under Roman dominance. Corinth was destroyed stone by stone when its leaders tried to defy Roman authority. The Romans also restricted trade, which the Greeks found necessary to compensate for their poor farmland. Money brought in by students and tourists from Rome helped Greece survive. Athens became, in today's phraseology, a "college town."

Roman rule over Greece lasted five hundred years. It ended with the decline of Rome. Shortly before Rome's fall, the seeds of a new state, which thrived largely because of the spirit and energy of the Greek people, were planted.

THE BYZANTINE EMPIRE

Byzantine culture grew out of the ancient Greek city of Byzantium (now Istanbul, Turkey). In 330, the Roman emperor Constantine the Great moved his capital to Byzantium. He renamed the city Constantinople in 331. When the western Roman Empire collapsed in the 470s, the East developed into what is called the Byzantine Civilization. Byzantine culture had both

*Ruins of the Temple of Athena Lindía in Rhodes, where
St. Paul the Apostle was said to have visited*

Roman and Greek roots, but the Greek influence was stronger.

Profound changes swept old Greece during the Byzantine period. The center of Greek culture shifted from Athens to Constantinople, called "New Rome." In the fourth and fifth centuries after Christ, many of the same barbarian tribes that had vanquished Rome swept onto mainland Greece and the islands. From the sixth to the tenth centuries, Slavic people migrated to Greek soil. These newcomers were assimilated with the ancient inhabitants.

Christianity became the official religion of the Byzantine Empire in 379. The graceful Greek temples, built a thousand years earlier, suffered during the conversion period. While the Roman conquerors generally respected the temples, the early Christians tore down dozens of them because they believed the structures to be an evil pagan influence.

Mosaics, the art form in which pieces of glass or colored stones

A mosaic in the interior of a Byzantine church

are pressed into mortar to form pictures, reached new heights during Byzantine times. Glittering mosaics, so intricate they astounded viewers, decorated church walls. Mosaic art never again achieved the lofty standards set by Byzantine masters.

The development of Byzantine art was disturbed in 726 when Emperor Leo III removed sacred images from churches because, he believed, they filled the worshiper's heads with superstition rather than true Christian faith. Religious art objects were called "icons," and those who favored removing or destroying them were known as "iconoclasts." Many church leaders objected to the destruction of religious art, and the conflict that developed shook the foundations of the empire. Today the word iconoclast is used to describe a person who attacks long-standing beliefs.

Church architecture was the crowning achievement of Byzantine culture. Byzantine churches featured a central dome supported by arches and standing on piers. The most famous example of a Byzantine church is the Hagia Sophia (Greek words meaning Holy Wisdom), which was built in the 530s and still stands in Istanbul.

The Great Schism (split) occurred in 1054, dividing the Christian church into two separate and hostile camps. The Eastern church, centered in Constantinople, and the Western church in Rome had been drifting apart for hundreds of years. Differences in religious philosophy and the Roman pope's claim to authority over the Eastern church led to their final separation. The Eastern church is called *orthodox* to emphasize that it follows the true faith. The modern Greek Orthodox church is part of that body.

The Byzantine Era lasted about one thousand years. The empire fell when Ottoman Turks conquered Constantinople in 1453. For Greece the period of captivity continued.

OTTOMAN RULE

The Ottoman Empire was centered in what is today the nation of Turkey, and Constantinople served as its capital. Although the Ottoman Turks were Muslims, they allowed their Christian subjects religious freedom. The Turks encouraged the Greeks to become Muslims, but conversion was not required. Most Greeks remained Christian.

Some Greek cities were given a form of self-government, but the Ottoman Turks imposed heavy taxes on their Christian subjects. Every non-Muslim in the empire was required to pay a yearly "head tax." It was called a head tax because anyone who failed to pay lost his head to the axe and block. The cruelest tax was that imposed on young boys. Every Christian family that produced two or more male children had to turn at least one son over to the Turks to be trained as a soldier. As a member of the Turkish army, the Greek usually became an enemy of fellow Greeks.

During Ottoman rule, hunger and hopelessness shrouded

El Greco's landscape of Toledo, Spain

Greece. People who could find the money emigrated to foreign shores. The Greek countryside became so empty that a British ambassador reported he could ride for up to six days without finding a village large enough to support him and his horse.

One Greek who fled his native land was the brilliant artist Domenikos Theotokopoulos. He studied in Italy and painted in Spain where he was known as El Greco (the Greek). El Greco broke artistic traditions by deliberately distorting light and form in order to make a personal statement. His landscape of the Spanish town of Toledo is one of history's famous paintings. El Greco died in 1614.

The Ottoman Empire waged a long series of wars with the Italian state of Venice, and Greece was often used as a battleground. During a clash in 1687, a Venetian cannonball dropped through the roof of the Parthenon and exploded amid barrels of gunpowder. The roof was blown to bits, dozens of intricate statues were shattered, and the building split almost in two. In one instant a treasure of the Golden Age was forever scarred.

The Turks ruled Greece for four hundred years. Cold and aloof, they called their Christian subjects *rayah* — the word means slave. Then, revolutions abroad fired Greek patriotism. In America, a weak colonial people broke the chains of British rule. In France, the peasants rose up against the ruling class. Freedom stirred the air, and after a period of sleep that lasted 2,200 years, the Greeks began to breathe.

INDEPENDENCE

On the 25th of March, 1821, Archbishop Germanos of the city of Patras raised a religious flag and proclaimed independence for Greece. The date is now celebrated as Greek Independence Day. The claim of independence meant very little, however, because the Turkish army still occupied the land. Greece won its freedom only after a long, bloody, and shockingly cruel war.

From out of the mountains rode Greek outlaw patriots, called *klephts*, who attacked Turkish soldiers and then melted into the night. Both sides fought with a passion and fury that degenerated into barbarism. Torture, the slaughter of civilians, and power lust among military leaders all played an ugly part in this war, which lasted from 1821 to 1829. Heroes emerged for the Greek side too.

AΚΛΙΝΗΚΕΝΗΦΕ
ΤΑΙΕΣΤΡΛΜΕΝΗ
ΝΑΦΑΝΛΝ

ΜΑΣ
ΙΑ
ΡΟΝ
ΛΛΠΑΚΙ

Greek soldiers, called evzoni, *dress in fezes, kilts, and shoes with turned-up toes and pompons. In the picture above they perform precise military movements in front of the Parliament building in Athens.*

According to a popular poem, a Greek threatened with death by torture told his Turkish jailers: "Go, you and your faith, you infidels, to destruction. I was born a Greek and a Greek I will die!"

True to the Greek character, the freedom fighters argued endlessly about the strategies and goals of their revolution. The educated soldiers remembered that the Greek army was once stopped at the gates of Troy because its officers were unable to agree on a plan of attack. Soon Greek revolutionaries fought each other as furiously as they fought the enemy.

As the fighting dragged on, Greek independence was heralded

in western Europe. European libertarians, still seized by the ideals of the French Revolution, revered ancient Athens for giving democracy to the world. The German poets Goethe and Schiller and the French writer Victor Hugo championed the Greek cause. In Great Britain the poets Byron and Shelley wrote glowing odes to Greece. Young European idealists volunteered to fight for Greek independence. The last letter of one Swiss volunteer serving in a besieged Greek city read, "I am proud to think that the blood of a Swiss, of a child of William Tell, is about to mingle with that of the heroes of Greece."

Finally the European governments entered the struggle. In October 1827, a joint French, British, and Russian fleet devastated the naval forces of Turkey and her Egyptian allies. A land war then broke out between Russia and the Ottoman Empire. To repel the Russians, the Ottoman Turks had to remove their forces from Greece. The Turkish retreat opened the land to the revolutionary forces. Throughout the Greek countryside rang the cry, "Freedom! Freedom! Freedom at last!"

No one expressed the sentiment of newfound Greek liberty more eloquently than the British poet Lord Byron, who died of a fever while serving in Greece. Shortly before his death, Byron stood at Marathón, the battleground where the ancient Greeks defeated their Persian enemies, and wrote:

> The mountains look on Marathon—
> And Marathon looks on the sea;
> And musing there an hour alone,
> I dream'd that Greece might still be free;
> For standing on the Persians' grave
> I could not deem myself a slave.

Chapter 7

THE MODERN STATE

Politically, modern Greece was born when the country achieved its independence from Turkey in 1829. Decades of hope, dismay, civil strife, and war followed before Greece was able to take its rightful place in the European community.

KINGSHIP AND THE GREAT IDEA

Newly independent Greece was a tiny, war-torn state of about 1.5 million people. Its land area included the central mainland, the Peloponnesus, and several nearby islands, making its territory about half the size of the present-day nation. Several million Greeks still lived in Turkey or on lands under Turkish control. The large number of Greeks living as Turkish subjects gave rise to a particular passion called the *Megale Idea*, or Great Idea. Believers in the Great Idea dreamed of uniting all Greeks in the Mediterranean world into one state.

Greece's first government was imposed on the country by its allies, Britain, France, and Russia. The allies believed the country needed a king to preserve order. They chose Otto, crown prince of

Otto (left) was forced from the throne in 1862 and replaced by George I (right).

the German state of Bavaria. Otto was a Roman Catholic, he spoke no Greek, and he was only seventeen when he accepted the throne in 1833. A peaceful uprising in 1844 forced Otto to accept a Parliament and a prime minister. A new revolt in 1862 removed him from the throne. Otto was replaced by the Danish prince George I, a competent and wise ruler who reigned for fifty years, from 1863 to 1913.

Two important visitors in the late 1800s were the archaeologists Heinrich Schliemann from Germany and Arthur Evans from England. Schliemann made significant discoveries at Mycenae and excavated Homer's Troy. Evans uncovered Minoan sites on the island of Crete. Before the work of these two men, scholars believed Greek history began with the Dorian invasion, and dismissed stories about earlier civilization as mere myths.

The Great Idea and the expansion of Greek territory remained a passionate issue. A war between Greece and Turkey broke out in

1897 over the status of Crete. The island was still held by the Turkish government, but its population was overwhelmingly Greek. In a series of battles that lasted about thirty days, the Greek armed forces suffered humiliating losses. Because of the defeats, debate in Parliament raged into fistfights and even gun duels.

Beginning in 1910, the brilliant statesman from Crete, Eleutherios Venizelos, served as prime minister. He was devoted to the Great Idea but hoped to expand Greek territory through alliances rather than wars that pitted Greece alone against Turkey. Allied with Bulgaria, Montenegro, and Serbia, Greece waged war against Turkey in 1912. A dissatisfied Bulgaria fought with its former allies in a second war. The two conflicts, called the "Balkan Wars," gave Greece Crete, the regions of Epirus and Macedonia, and most of the Aegean Islands.

WORLD WAR I

In 1914, Europe plunged into the bloodiest war in its history. At the war's beginnings, Prime Minister Venizelos urged the government to join the Allies against Germany and her Axis partners, one of which was Turkey. But the king's family had ties to German royalty and he kept the country neutral. Venizelos orchestrated a revolution, King Constantine was exiled, and Greece entered the war on the side of the Allies. World War I ended in 1918. The peace treaty gave Greece the region of Thrace, but the statesman Venizelos wanted more. To him the Great Idea meant the building of a Greek empire in Asia Minor with Constantinople as its capital. He believed the many Greeks living in Turkey would make that dream a reality.

Venizelos sent troops against Turkey in 1919, but the war-

King Constantine

weary people of Greece forced the prime minister out of office and recalled King Constantine. The king, however, would hear no talk of retreat. He launched a do-or-die campaign aimed at final victory. Greece teetered on the brink of either realizing the full scope of the Great Idea or suffering a humiliating defeat at the hands of its ancient enemies.

THE CATASTROPHE OF ASIA MINOR

Early in the military campaign, Greek forces penetrated deep into Turkey. Commanding the Turkish army was the crafty Kemal Ataturk, who allowed the Greeks to advance far enough to strain their supply lines before he launched a major attack. Fifty thousand Greek soldiers were killed, wounded, or captured. Turkish troops then turned on the peaceful Greek villages of Asia

Joannes Metaxas is remembered for saying "no" or "ochi" to the Italian Fascist leader Benito Mussolini. "Ochi Day" is celebrated on October 28.

Minor, looting, burning, and slaughtering civilians. The blood spilled on the shores of Turkey shattered the Great Idea dream forever.

Under terms of the peace treaty, 1.3 million Greeks were forced to leave Asia Minor and move permanently to Greece. Also, 400,000 Turks living in Greek territory were required to resettle in Turkey. The sudden influx of more than a million people put an impossible strain on the already weak Greek economy. Old people still tell tales of the hunger, homelessness, and disease that swept Greece during that bitter time. Yet the exchange of people removed the chief cause of hostility between Greeks and Turks, at least for the time being.

WORLD WAR II AND ITS AFTERMATH

In the 1930s, power fell to a military dictator named Joannes Metaxas. He was a great admirer of the Italian Fascist leader Benito Mussolini. On an October night in 1940, the Italian

*In 1941 German tanks rumbled into Lárisa (left) and the rest of Greece,
and raised their flag over the Acropolis (right) in Athens.*

ambassador knocked on Metaxas' door and demanded immediate
permission to build bases on Greek soil. Metaxas, who was still in
his pajamas, looked at the Italian and said simply, *"Ochi."* The
word means "no." October 28 is now a national patriotic holiday
called "Ochi Day."

War between Greece and Italy began within hours. To the
astonishment of world leaders, poorly armed Greek troops
whipped the Italian army, which was equipped with modern
weapons. Mussolini suffered a loss of prestige from which he
never recovered. In the spring of 1941, Adolf Hitler came to the
aid of his Italian ally. The Greeks were unable to turn back waves
of German tanks and dive bombers, and the country fell.
Newspapers around the world printed a picture filled with grim
irony. The Nazi swastika, a symbol of tyranny, fluttered above the
Acropolis where democracy was born.

The Germans soon discovered that Greeks fight with the
ferocity of lions against foreign overlords. In the early 1940s, the
Greek underground became the most effective of all resistance
movements in Nazi-occupied Europe. The Germans executed

hundreds of civilians, hoping to discourage the guerrilla warriors. But, as had been true so often in the past, the freedom fighters were a divided lot. Some (called Royalists) wanted to live under a king when the Germans were defeated; others wanted a Communist government. Soon the country was wracked by a confusing three-way war, in which Greek factions fought against each other and against the Germans all at the same time.

German occupying troops were transferred to other fronts in 1944. By then, the civil war between Royalists and Communists raged everywhere. British troops landed near Athens and found themselves firing upon the city they had come to liberate.

For the Greeks, the end of World War II brought only temporary relief from bloodshed. A new and even bloodier civil war broke out in 1946. The United States poured money and arms to the Royalist side to prevent the Communists from winning. Communist resistance finally collapsed in 1949. Between World War II and the civil war, one in ten Greeks had died either in combat or from starvation.

RECOVERY

In the 1950s, Greece was hailed as a paradise for struggling writers and artists looking for a cheap place to live. A house in a fishing village rented for $20 a month and a maid was willing to work for $2 a week. In the town square, boys fought each other for the privilege of shining a foreigner's shoes for a nickel. This was part of Greece's long and sometimes degrading path toward economic recovery.

The Americans continued their aid program, because they feared the Greek people would turn to communism if they saw no relief from poverty. The economy expanded largely due to advances in the shipping industry. Starting with war surplus American freighters, the Greek merchant marine became one of the world's strongest fleets. Tourism also grew, and demand for new hotels touched off a building boom in Athens.

The government faced a nagging problem on the British island colony of Cyprus. The population of the island was 80 percent Greek and 20 percent Turkish. Greek Cypriots wanted their island to join Greece. Turkey and the Turkish Cypriots objected. Cyprus became an independent nation in 1960, but the future of the island remained a sore point between Greece and Turkey.

THE COLONELS

In April 1967, the world was stunned by a military takeover of the Greek government. A correspondent from *Time* magazine reported, "Moments after midnight, moving so fast that it all seemed over in minutes, shadowy figures in battle dress began to appear everywhere. . . . From the lovely plains of Lakonia to the forbidding hills of Macedonia, Greece quickly found itself under the grip of a new master: the army."

The military coup was the work of three obscure army officers who were known to the world press as "the colonels." They claimed the fabric of Greek government was being eroded due to constant clashes between Prime Minister George Papandreou and King Constantine II. The colonels maintained that the country needed the firm hand of military rule until a workable civilian government could be formed. The highest ranking colonel explained, "If the patient is not strapped to the table, the surgeon cannot perform a successful operation."

Tanks stood in Omonoia Square (left) in 1973 when Greece was under martial law.
Right: Andreas Papandreou (left) meets with NATO Secretary General Lord Carrington in 1986.

In the first few weeks of military rule, thousands of people the colonels deemed to be troublemakers were thrown in jail. Among those arrested was Andreas Papandreou, the son of the prime minister and a budding politician. The military rulers limited the authority of Parliament, forbade criticism in the press, and virtually stripped the king of power. The colonels remained in power for seven years, and Greece suffered the stigma of having the only military dictatorship in western Europe during the post-war years.

Events on the troubled island of Cyprus led to the colonels' fall. Turkey raced troops to the island after a Greek revolt there in 1974. Afraid to confront the Turkish army, the military government resigned. Although the Greeks lost prestige, the people celebrated the final end of the military government. An eyewitness in Athens' Syntagma (Constitution) Square said, "People swarmed over the square, exploding into cheers and chants of hilarious celebration. Greek flags appeared out of nowhere."

GREECE TODAY

The Greek people held a new election in 1974 and, by a two-to-one margin, voted to end their 140-year-old monarchy. Greece became a republic. In the same election, the Greeks chose Constantine Karamanlis as their prime minister.

Greece became a member of the European Economic Community (EEC) in 1981. The EEC is a group of western European nations that attempt to unite all their resources into one strong economy. Joining the EEC was an important step, because it assured Greece of its place in the family of western states.

Also in 1981, the Greek Socialist party won a landslide victory and gained control of the Parliament. Andreas Papandreou, the son of the past prime minister, led the Socialists. He was reelected prime minister in 1985 when his party won 45 percent of the vote.

To western European allies, and especially to the United States, Andreas Papandreou is an enigma. He was once an American citizen, his English is flawless, and his wife was born in the United States. Yet he delights in defying the United States. Once in office, Papandreou made a billion-dollar trade agreement with Libya's Colonel Qaddafi, whom the United States condemns as a terrorist. Papandreou's speeches tend to be anti-American and pro-Soviet.

In the mid-1980s, Greece suffered severe economic reversals. Shipping and tourism, which provide tens of thousands of jobs, slumped. Unemployment doubled in the first half of the 1980s, and many Greeks who kept their jobs worked only two or three days a week. Experts worry about the fate of Greek democracy if the economy remains in a tailspin through the 1990s.

Worry beads, said to help relieve tension, can be purchased just about anywhere. The former Royal Palace in Syntagma Square (below) is the seat of Parliament.

Chapter 8

THE GOVERNMENT
AND THE ECONOMY

Greek males have a peculiar habit of twirling strings of beads called *kombologia*, or "worry beads." They claim the practice relieves tension. Taxi drivers swing their beads when caught in a traffic jam, and students fondle them while waiting to take an exam. The state of the economy and the condition of government are always causes of tension in Greece. Unemployment, which today affects tens of thousands of persons, is causing a boom in the sale of worry beads.

THE GOVERNMENT

Greece's proper name is the Hellenic Republic. The nation has two chief executive officers, the president and the prime minister. The president serves as the head of the state, while the prime minister heads the government. In day-to-day operations, the prime minister is the more powerful officer. The prime minister leads the majority party in Parliament, and this position enables him to set government policy. Sometimes the president and the prime minister are at loggerheads with each other.

A political demonstration in Athens

Parliament consists of three hundred members who are elected to four-year terms. The Parliament, called the *Vouli,* has no upper or lower houses, so all deputies cast an equal vote. One of its most important functions is to prepare the annual budget for the country.

Greek law allows close cooperation between church and state. Classes in the Greek Orthodox religion are held in all public schools. Still, the constitution guarantees all people the freedom of worship, and Jewish synagogues, Muslim mosques, and rival Christian churches function in the country.

At enormous cost, Greece maintains a modern army, navy, and air force. All able-bodied men must serve a two-year term in one of the armed services. Government leaders claim the danger of war with Turkey requires the nation to spend money on arms, but a strong military is worrisome for the politicians. No one forgets that as recently as 1967 the military took over the government, and that Greece has had a long and depressing history of similar military uprisings.

POLITICAL GREECE

Graffiti mars the walls of Athens' buildings. Most of the scribblings are political messages, and it is not necessary to know the Greek language to interpret them. The Communist party spray paints in red, the Conservatives in black, the Socialists in green, and the Democrats in blue. This kaleidoscope is all part of the passion of Greek politics.

Arguing politics is a national mania. In Athens' Omonoia and Syntagma squares, political debaters stand in groups of ten to fifteen, mostly men, shouting, waving their arms, stamping their feet, doing anything to drive a point home. Also, Athens has at least a dozen daily newspapers, each of which slants toward a slightly different political position. Readers buy their papers and argue politics at the newsstands.

Some Greeks pray for the day when a courageous leader will unite citizens of all political persuasions and send the country marching to the beat of a single drummer. However, as former Prime Minister Constantine Karamanlis recently said, "In our day there are no messiahs, and if by chance we think we have found one, it will not be long before we turn on him. So we Greeks have been since ancient times. We are skillful at making idols, not that we may worship them, but that we may have the pleasure of destroying them."

EDUCATION

Greek law requires all children to attend at least nine years of school. At age six, the child starts at an elementary school called *demotiko*. After six years, the student begins a three-year course at

Athens University

the *gymnasio*. Next comes a final three years of study at the *lycio*.
Classes through all grades are free. Textbooks are also free and the
student is allowed to keep them upon completion of a grade.
There are very few private schools in Greece. Even the sons and
daughters of the upper classes attended public schools.

Since the 1970s, mandatory school laws have been enforced
throughout the country. Rarely does one meet a young Greek who
cannot read or write. In the past, however, school laws were
neglected in the rural areas. Many farm families believed sending
a girl to school was unnecessary, or even immoral. Consequently,
Greece has an adult illiteracy rate that is high by western
European standards. Women make up the great majority of adults
who cannot read or write.

To be admitted into a university, a lycio graduate must pass a
rigorous series of tests. Once admitted, though, the university
student pays no tuition, all books are free, and the universities
provide meals and dormitory beds. Many older Greeks, who pay
taxes for these services, grumble about "professional students"
who remain in college even though they are in their thirties.

The sea is vital to Greece.
Fishermen (left) pull in their nets.
Sponges (right) are another product from the sea.

THE ECONOMY

The Greek economy lags behind those of other western European nations. Poor farmland, scarce natural resources, and a late start at manufacturing are the primary reasons for the disparity. Clothing and processed foods are the major goods produced by the private economy. Despite a dramatic increase in manufacturing and factory construction during the 1960s and 1970s, Greece is forced to import almost twice the value of goods that it exports.

Agriculture employs almost 30 percent of the Greek work force. Most of these workers are small farmers who, by heroic effort, grow grapes, olives, and vegetables on their tiny farms. Many villages are dependent upon fishing. Every morning, hardy fishermen can be seen at the waterfront readying their nets. The men sadly ply their trade on the already overfished and badly polluted Mediterranean Sea.

Some Greeks, such as Aristotle Onassis (right), made a fortune in the shipping industry. Left: A container ship at the port of Piraeus

Since natural resources are meager, the mining industry generates few jobs. A low-grade coal called lignite is mined in the Peloponnesus and in the northern mountains. Lignite is burned mainly in power plants to generate electricity. Bauxite, used to make aluminum, is also mined in Greece.

By the mid-1980s, the Greek merchant fleet totaled 3,700 major vessels and ranked second largest in the world. "One-tenth of all Greek families live directly or indirectly from shipping," says the president of the Union of Greek Ship Owners. In recent years the number of ships throughout the world has exceeded the demand for shipping. Profits in the once-lucrative shipping industry have dropped sharply. By 1986, 20 percent of all Greek ships were lying idle in harbors. Meanwhile, their sailors sat on the waterfront twirling worry beads.

The wealthy Greeks can afford to own private pleasure ships (left), while others are not as well off. Many earn money by selling their home-grown vegetables at city markets. Above, beans are picked over, to ready them for sale.

THE RICH AND THE POOR

During the 1930s, the young businessman Aristotle Onassis scraped together enough money to buy two leaky, rust-covered freighters. After World War II, Onassis added secondhand American freighters to his fleet. He was soon one of the world's richest men. In 1968, he became an international celebrity when he married Jacqueline Kennedy, widow of the American president.

Like Onassis, most Greek millionaires are self-made. Even families that were rich in the distant past lost their fortunes during World War II and the civil war, and had to start over with practically nothing. Until recent years there was very little inherited wealth in Greece. Perhaps for this reason the Greek poor tend to respect rather than envy the rich.

The legions of poor people maintain their lives with remarkable dignity. Rarely does one see a beggar or even a person who appears ill-fed or poorly clothed. A man or a woman can wander

Garlic for sale at a market in Athens

through the most impoverished neighborhood in Athens and never worry about being robbed or attacked. Drug and alcohol abuse, which ravage poor communities in other countries, hardly exist in Greece. Yet many people live off the welfare system, which provides temporary help for destitute families. Greek fathers, who grew up under the philotimo creed that demands that a man provide for his family regardless of circumstances, sometimes hide their faces when they are forced to stand in the welfare line.

TOURISM

Tourism is the nation's major industry. Through the early 1980s, five million people visited Greece each year and spent,

Because there is so much to see in Greece, such as the ancient Acropolis in Athens (left) and quaint islands (right), tourism is a major industry.

collectively, two billion dollars. Hotels, restaurants, and other tourist-related enterprises employ more Greek workers than does any other business.

The 1986 season was a disaster, as tourists, especially Americans, shunned Europe out of fear of terrorism and avoided Greece because of a 1985 hijacking at the Athens airport that left one passenger dead. Airport security became a hotly debated political issue in Greece. Security was tightened at Athens and the International Air Transport Association later claimed it was "one of the safest [airports] in the world."

If fear of terrorism subsides, the 1986 drought will be forgotten. If not, the Greek economy faces even greater woes in the future. Some merchants are stocking up their supply of worry beads.

The open-air theater on the Acropolis in Athens, completed by the Romans in 161 B.C., is still used for performances.

Chapter 9

ARTS AND ENTERTAINMENT

Greece can be many things, but it is never dull. The people see to that. In the daytime, one can enjoy the many museums and art galleries. At night, a world of entertainment opens to charm both visitor and native.

LITERATURE AND THE THEATER

In the modern era two Greek poets have received Nobel prizes for literature. George Seferis won the award in 1963, and Odysseus Elytis gained his Nobel Prize in 1979. Seferis, who is also a diplomat, writes poems that lament the tragic periods of Greek history. The national poet is Dionysios Solomos who, during the early 1800s, wrote in the language of the common people.

Nikos Kazantzakis enjoys the greatest international following of any modern Greek writer. His novel *Zorba the Greek* was translated into a dozen languages and made into a popular movie. Kazantzakis also wrote works that penetrate deep into religious and philosophical realms. His lyric poem "The Odyssey: a Modern Sequel" continues the ancient tale from the point where Homer ended his story. Kazantzakis' *The Last Temptation of Christ* and *Christ Recrucified* are works of mystical interest.

Alexandros Papadiamadis gained fame writing stories about village life. His short novel *The Murderess* is hailed as a masterwork. Andreas Karkavitsas also wrote moving short stories about life in rural and maritime Greece. A starkly realistic novel called *The Beggar* is his greatest achievement.

More than one hundred legitimate theaters operate in Athens alone. Demand for theater space is so great that stages and seats have been hammered together in garages, warehouses, and abandoned factory buildings. In the countryside, open-air theaters, built more than 2,000 years ago, are still used to stage dramas written by Sophocles and Euripides.

During popular street shows, the audience watches shadows cast by dancing puppets. The puppeteer mouths the words of his characters and creates sound effects. Children enjoy shadow shows because they are charged with constant action and movement. The stories contain historic and political messages designed to capture the interest of parents. A common figure in the shows is the puppet *Karagiozis,* who lived during the period of Turkish occupation and delights in outwitting and outfighting Turkish policemen.

MOVIES AND TELEVISION

Practically all Greeks grumble about the quality of their movies and television programs. Both industries are carefully regulated by the government. The bureau that oversees movies acts as a censor and severely limits the amount of money that can be spent on film production. Greek scriptwriters are notoriously underpaid and many plots are either boring or confusing.

Television suffers from government control even more than

Left: Dancers in traditional dress   Right: A musician entertains at a sidewalk taverna.

does the film industry. Viewers complain that newscasters ignore world events and simply report whatever the ruling party in Parliament orders. Dramatic shows seem to have a bleak sameness. Most Greeks watch foreign dramatic shows that are dubbed into the Greek language. Through the 1980s, the American series "Dallas" was a hit even though Greek college graduates often apologized when they admitted to watching it.

MUSIC AND DANCE

Music to fit all tastes is available in Athens. A person can attend a Mozart chamber concert, listen to a jazz group from New Orleans, or catch a blaring rock band.

Closer to the Greek soul is folk music accompanied by the stringed instrument called the *bouzouki*. Resembling a mandolin, the bouzouki blends well with folk songs that are either joyous or sorrowful. *Rebetika* is a particular style of mournful music usually sung to the accompaniment of the bouzouki. Rebetika songs were

83

*An artist painting pottery (left) and a view of
ancient art (right) in the National Museum in Athens*

brought to Greece by homeless refugees from Asia Minor in the
1920s. The songs, haunting and hypnotic, could be compared to
the blues introduced by black Americans at almost the same time.

On festival days, villagers dance arm in arm around the town
square. Men dance with men, women with women, or men and
women dance alone. "When the music strikes you, who needs a
partner?" asks a village fisherman. The most common solo dance
is called the *zeibekiko*. Foreigners often try to dance the zeibekiko,
but quickly discover it is not as easy as it looks. Greek folk
dancing requires a rare blend of precision and soul.

THE FINE ARTS

"When I first started painting, everything was colorful. Then I
went to Paris and my bright colors disappeared . . . I used reddish,
not red. When I came back to Greece the light went on. I used
color again." So reports the Greek artist Kostas Paniaras. Like
hundreds of other Greek artists he spent years studying and
working abroad, but came home in the 1980s. The returning
artists are making the Greek art scene one of the liveliest in
Europe. Athens abounds with art galleries. The National Gallery

in Athens holds modern paintings that are revered by art lovers around the world.

Most people find post-World War II Greek architecture disappointing. The modern section of Athens is a city where one concrete-and-glass canyon invariably winds into another with monotonous predictability. However, Athens contains an exhausting number of ancient and medieval sites that warm the heart of architecture connoisseurs.

SPORTS

Taxi drivers claim the only time Athens' streets are not choking in a sea of cars is when the Greek national soccer team plays an important game on television. But it is a mystery how the drivers know this, since they too abandon their cabs to crowd around a TV set during such games. Soccer, or *podosphero*, is a passion in Greece.

In addition to international competition, Greece has a professional league made up of sixteen soccer teams. The most popular are the Panathinaikos of Athens and their arch-rivals the Olympiakos of neighboring Piraeus. Both teams are owned by wealthy shipowners who try to outdo each other by paying lavish salaries to top players (shades of American baseball). Amateur soccer is popular, too. The sport is played by six-year-old demotiko pupils as well as university students.

Basketball is the country's second favorite team sport. It is played in all the school levels and is a favorite among Greek girls.

Greece gave the world the Olympic Games in ancient times. In 1896 the first modern Olympic Games were held in Athens. Some members of the International Olympic Committee want the

*A buffet of Greek food (above) may include
dried octopus (top left) and grilled goat
meat (bottom left) and is sure to be delicious.*

Games to be held every four years in Greece, instead of skipping
from country to country. Greeks applaud the idea, but it has never
gone beyond the discussion stage.

FOOD AND DRINK

Like Chinese and Italian cuisine, Greek food is so relished it has
crossed oceans and leaped continents. The favorite dishes are
known practically everywhere; *moussaka*, layers of eggplant and
ground meat baked in a tangy sauce; *souvlakia*, cubes of lamb or
pork and vegetables strung on a long needle and roasted over a
fire; *dolmathes*, rice and ground meat wrapped in vine leaves;
soupa augolemono, chicken soup with lemon flavoring; and *baklava*,
a dessert made of pastry and nuts and coated with honey.

Lamb is the Greeks' favorite meat, and spinach is their preferred vegetable. Being people of the sea, Greeks serve endless varieties of fish dishes. Almost all their food is cooked in olive oil. Two generations ago it was said that a fragrant cloud of olive oil hung over Athens. Now all one smells in the city is car fumes.

Fun spots to eat are the restaurants called tavernas. They display their food under glass and on top of a table, so the patrons can pick what they wish to eat. Taverna food is served lukewarm, never hot. This frustrates Americans and northern Europeans who like their food steaming, but the Greeks claim the cooler temperature brings out the flavor better.

Most Greeks drink wine with their meals. A common white wine, called *retsina*, is mixed with pine resin. Outsiders complain it tastes like kerosene, but Greeks say it helps one digest rich, oily foods. For the most part, Greeks drink wine, beer, or a spirit called *ouzo* only with meals. Belting down drinks without eating anything is almost unheard-of. Perhaps for that reason one seldom sees a drunken man or woman stumbling about the streets.

FESTIVALS

Christmas tends to be a quiet, but certainly not solemn, season. On the evenings between Christmas and New Year's, children sing carols from house to house and collect bits of food and pieces of candy. St. Basil's Day (which is celebrated on New Year's Day) is a time for parties and gift giving. On Twelfth Night (January 5), the village priest blesses fields and houses. The next day is Epiphany, which commemorates Christ's baptism in the Jordan River. In some villages, the priest celebrates Epiphany by

A celebration for the feast of St. Spyridon

throwing a cross into the sea, and, while the whole town watches, village boys dive to retrieve it.

Instead of birthdays, most Greeks celebrate their "name day," or the feast day of their patron saint. For example, on St. George's Day everyone named George celebrates his name day by welcoming his friends at home. Upon arriving at George's house, custom demands the guests utter a simple two-word greeting, "Many years."

No time of year is more important to the Greek soul than the Easter season. The Eastern Orthodox churches celebrate the events of Easter one week later than the Western churches. The season begins with Carnival, a riotous party night when everyone stuffs themselves with food and drink as a final fling before the long lean days of Lent. During Carnival, children are allowed (and encouraged) to wander the streets bashing adults wth long sausage-like balloons. Lent officially begans on *Kathari Deftera*, or Clean Monday, when families bring very simple foods out to the country and have a picnic. At the picnic the kids busy themselves flying kites.

During the forty days of Lent, a devout Greek will shun meat, olive oil, and wine. Good Friday is a day of total fast and only essential workers show up at their jobs. Churches are draped in black, and their bells toll solemnly. The entire nation falls into a deep state of gloom that, to foreigners, is disturbingly real.

Near midnight on Holy Saturday a special and very moving church service is held. The service begins with the priest reading the words of St. Paul to the Greeks at Corinth: "Listen! I will unfold a mystery—we shall not all die, but we shall all be changed in a flash, in the twinkling of an eye, at the last trumpet call. For the trumpet will sound, and the dead will rise immortal, and we shall be changed."

After the reading, the lights inside the church dim, and for a few seconds an eerie silence envelops the congregation. At the stroke of midnight the priest lights a fresh candle.and announces in a voice filled with joy: *"Christos anesti!"* (Christ is risen!) The parishoners respond: *"Alithos anesti!"* (Indeed He has risen!) The people then stream toward the altar and light candles from the priest's candle. Carrying their flickering candles, they march out of church into a night that is alive with bells pealing wildly and fireworks exploding in the sky. *"Christos anesti!"* they cry to neighbors and strangers alike. *"Alithos anesti!"* comes the reply.

The season of sorrows has ended. The Greek people now look forward to a bountiful Easter Sunday dinner, and to the start of a fresh new spring.

Above: Rugged limestone mountains north of Athens   Below: A view of Thessaloníki, a commercial and industrial center of the north, which is built on a hill

Chapter 10

A TOUR OF GREECE

For a land so small, Greece presents the visitor with an amazing array of sights—craggy mountains, lonely seacoasts, and patchwork farms. The nation has a large, noisy city and dozens of towns and villages that hold special charms. And in Greece, the past is always present. Throughout the country stand monuments testifying to an age of glory.

THE NORTH

The principal region in northern Greece is Macedonia. Unlike most of the nation's parched land, Macedonia has fertile plains and rushing rivers that make it one of the major "breadbaskets" of Greece.

The seaport of Thessaloníki (also called Salonika) is Macedonia's leading city. Thessaloníki was named after the sister of Alexander the Great. It is the nation's second-largest city. Thessaloníki has an old section made up of a maze of twisting narrow streets flanked by the bare walls of tiny houses. Many of the old city's buildings and churches were constructed in Byzantine times. The famous White Tower of Thessaloníki was

The waterfront of Thessaloníki, with the White Tower in the background

built around 1430 and served as a fortress to ward off invaders. An archaeological museum in the city displays treasures of Macedonian history.

On a finger of land jutting into the sea near Thessaloníki rises holy Mount Athos. It is a separate state occupied by Greek Orthodox monks who live in about twenty monasteries that cling to cliffs overlooking the sea. A law passed in 1060, which is still in effect, excludes women from even approaching the holy mountain. The ban extends even to female animals. Tour boats that contain women are forbidden to come closer than 500 yards (457 meters) of the monastery cliffs.

Rising between Macedonia and the region called Thessaly is mystical Mount Olympus, whose peaks are often shrouded by clouds. The earliest peoples of Greece believed twelve major gods lived in splendid castles atop this mountain.

One of the monasteries on the rocks of Meteora can be seen on the left.

CENTRAL GREECE

At the northern end of the Thessaly Plain stand the rocks of
Meteora, which burst out of the surrounding flatlands with
dramatic suddenness and from a distance look as forbidding as the
face of the moon. Geologists tell us these unusual formations were
carved out millions of years ago when the land was submerged
under ocean waters. In medieval times, monks, hoping to escape
the troubles of the world, lived prayerful lives in caves on the
rugged peaks. Over the years the holy men built monasteries on
the heights. The monasteries and their treasures of artwork can be
seen by anyone wishing to climb tortuous footpaths. In the old
days visitors had to be hoisted up to the peaks by a winch and
rope.

To the ancients, the oracle at Delphi occupied a holy place
where mere mortals communicated with the gods. It is set in a
cleft of Mt. Parnassos, thousands of feet above the Corinthian

The Temple of Athena at Delphi

Gulf. Sheer, multicolored cliffs rise above it on three sides, and below the lush green of sacred olive groves trails off into the misty blue of the gulf. No wonder the Greeks thought of Delphi as the *omphalos* (navel) of the world—its very center.

A vast temple complex was built on this sacred spot. The gods spoke to pilgrims first through a village woman who claimed to breathe divine gases emitting from the earth, and then through the priests who protected the site. The priests' words were always stated in the most general of terms, so it was impossible to prove that the advice of the oracle was wrong. For more than one thousand years, the oracle gave its visitors what they hoped was a glimpse into the future.

The modern town of Delphi, which lies near the ruins, is a village whose single main street is lined with souvenir shops and tourist restaurants. The ancient site contains the crumbling remains of the oracle buildings, an open-air theater built in Classical times, and a modern museum. Where the Acropolis

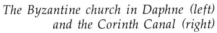
The Byzantine church in Daphne (left)
and the Corinth Canal (right)

impresses visitors with the majesty of ancients, the ruins of Delphi moves people with the mysticism that surrounded the society.

Near the Aegean Sea and north of Athens stands the church at Daphne. Dating from the eleventh century, the church is a sparkling example of the Byzantine Era. The walls are covered with delicate paintings and mosaics. Black-robed priests still tend to the churchyard's gardens, which are shaded by lovely groves of cypress trees.

THE PELOPONNESUS

The first imposing sight one encounters while driving from central Greece to the Peloponnesian Peninsula is the 3-mile- (4.8-kilometer-) long Corinth Canal. Digging a canal through the strait that leads to the Peloponnesus was a dream of the ancients, but work did not begin on the project until 1882. It took an army of laborers eleven years to complete the canal. The Corinth Canal

A street in Nauplion

makes the Peloponnesian landmass an island instead of a
peninsula.

Near the canal stand the ruins of ancient Corinth. There is little
remaining of this city, one of the richest city-states of antiquity.
During ancient times, the region near Corinth served as an
overland canal. Ships were partially disassembled, hoisted from
the water, and pushed over the strait on a trolleylike device.
Sections of the trolley's roadbed still exist.

Nauplion is one of the prettiest seacoast towns in all the
Peloponnesus. It boasts a quiet waterfront and houses built on
stepping-stones that rise from the sea. Although it attracts hordes
of tourists, the town maintains an unspoiled atmosphere. Legends
say it was founded by Nauplius, the son of the sea god Poseidon.
It was an important seaport for ancient Mycenae. In the 1830s
Nauplion served briefly as the capital city of the newly
independent Greek nation.

Just a short drive from Nauplion is the open-air theater of
Epidaurus. Built in the 400s B.C., the bow-like structure that is

Left: The theater of Epidaurus can seat fifteen thousand people.
Right: The ruins at Mycenae

carved into a hillside still functions as a theater. Its acoustics are so fine that a person sitting in the last row of seats—fully one hundred yards (ninety-one meters) from the center stage—can hear the actors breathing. In the 1970s, the Greek-American soprano Maria Callas sang operatic arias at Epidaurus and sent the audience away in tears of happiness.

The ancient city of Mycenae is one of the most famous archaeological sites in Greece. When Heinrich Schliemann began digging there in 1876, only the distinctive A-shaped "Lion's Gate" protruded above the shifting sands. Today, visitors climb about a sprawling complex of ruins that spreads over several acres. Prominent among the ruins are the beehive tombs dug into hills. Schliemann believed one of the largest of these tombs was the grave of Agamemnon, King of Mycenae and a leading figure in the *Iliad*.

The village of Olympia, where the ancient Olympic Games

At Olympia, the athletes ran under this arch when they entered the stadium from an underground passage.

began in 776 B.C., was a holy place for the Greeks. Over the years the ancients constructed public buildings and an imposing temple there. The statue of Zeus, magnificently carved in gold and ivory by the sculptor Phidias, used to stand in the temple. It was one of the Seven Wonders of the Ancient World. Earthquakes destroyed most of the buildings and early Christian zealots wrecked the temple. The marvelous statue of Zeus disappeared in the early Christian era. Today Olympia is another historic site popular with tourists. The starting and finishing stones of the great foot race still protrude above the grass of the stadium. Young visitors enjoy racing the full distance, which covers about 100 meters (109 yards).

Patras is the principal city of the Peloponnesus, and the fourth-largest urban center in the nation. Dominating its skyline are two interesting churches, both of which are dedicated to St. Andrew,

*The island of Corfu is a popular resort town in both
summer and winter. Right: Banners hang from balconies for a
special celebration.   Left: Narrow streets in the old section*

the patron saint of the city. Patras has a special place in modern
Greek history because it was there that Archbishop Germanos
proclaimed independence on the 25th of March in 1821.

THE ISLANDS

One of the highlights of a visitor's tour in Greece is a cruise to
the islands that dot the country's adjacent seas. Among the largest
of the islands in the Ionian Sea are Corfu, Cephalonia, Ithaca, and
Zante. About 183,000 people live on the Ionians. Agriculture and
tourism are the major industries.

Corfu is the most northerly of the Ionians. Its capital city boasts
buildings that are little changed since the days when Venetians
and Turks fought sea battles in the surrounding waters. The city's
focal point is the red-domed Church of St. Spyridon, built in 1589.

Overlooking the port of Piraeus

Islanders believe this church enjoys divine protection. During
World War II an air raid destroyed one-third of Corfu's buildings.
The Church of St. Spyridon was hit squarely on the roof by a
heavy bomb, but the bomb failed to explode.

The island of Levkás holds a festival of art and literature every
summer that attracts hundreds of people. The islanders also make
and sell beautiful lace embroideries. The nearby island of Ithaca
was the home of the wandering hero Odysseus, the central
character in Homer's poem, the *Odyssey*.

At the tip of the mainland are three islands—Aegina, Poros, and
Hydra—which are so close to the Athenian port of Piraeus that
vacationers can cruise to all three in a single day. Aegina's history
goes back to the legendary age when, it is said, Zeus turned the
ants of the island into people. Poros has long been a favorite
haunt for writers. The American author Henry Miller once said,

Poros (above left) and Hydra (right) are nestled in the blue Aegean Sea. Bottom left: Donkeys are used for transporting goods on Hydra.

"Coming into Poros gives the illusion of a deep dream." Hydra is the most charming of the three islands, largely because no cars or trucks are allowed there. A tourist can stroll the quiet streets or country trails and not worry about meeting a vehicle larger or faster than a donkey cart.

The sparkling blue Aegean Sea has 130 islands large enough to support inhabitants. The Aegean civilization of old predated that of mainland Greece.

The island of Páros is part of the south Aegean island group called the Cyclades. It is famed for its sunny climate and its long silvery beaches. Many of its older churches and buildings are made of a dazzling white marble.

In antiquity, the island of Rhodes housed a society of artists, poets, and philosophers. Two centuries before Christ, the people of Rhodes built a marvelous statue on their waterfront. Dedicated

At the entrance to a small harbor on Rhodes are two columns with bronze deer (left), the symbolic animals of Rhodes. The town of Líndhos (right) on Rhodes has a fortress built in the fifteenth century.

to the sun god, it rose as high as New York's Statue of Liberty. This "Colossus of Rhodes" was one of the Seven Wonders of the Ancient World, but was toppled by an earthquake shortly after its completion. Today, Rhodes is one of the most enchanting of the Aegean islands and a favorite tourist spot. Present-day visitors are greeted by two elegantly fashioned bronze deer that stand atop pillars facing the waterfront.

Sámos, which is separated from Turkey by a two-mile-wide (3.2-kilometer) strait, is one of the few Aegean islands that have patches of thick woods. Sámos has an attractive port city, Pythagorio, named after the mathematician and philosopher Pythagoras. Chios and Lesbos are two other large islands that lie so close to Turkey that islanders can see the Turkish coast from their hills. Traditions claim that Chios is the birthplace of Homer.

A panoramic view of Crete (above) and the market in the capital city of Iráklion (below)

Crete is the largest of all the Greek islands. It is famed for its inviting climate, its varied landscape, and its historic sites. Cretans have their own traditions in music, dance, and food. Foreigners sometimes complain they lack the refinements of mainland Greece. "Our ways are the ways of the mountain you see before you," said a Cretan shepherd. "I suppose we sometimes appear rough and illiterate, but our old people still recite by heart the verses of the *Odyssey*. Our women still retain customs that go back to the palaces of King Minos. They are the best mothers and wives in the world."

Crete has lovely seaport towns, such as Aghios Nikolaos and Elounta. Its largest city, Iráklion, is a busy, noisy commercial center. Its inland mountains harbor picturesque shepherd villages where time seems to have stood still.

The palace at Knossus

More than five thousand years ago, the Minoan civilization was centered at Knossus in Crete's highlands. The ruins of Knossus attract thousands of visitors each year. Legends claim the great god Zeus was born on Crete. Archaeologists are now making interesting discoveries by digging into the cave that was supposed to be Zeus' birthplace.

ATHENS

Athens marks the beginning and the end of most tours of Greece. The city shows the visitor two faces, the new and the old. The new face is marred by the screeching of tires, the blaring of horns, and the unrelenting roar of traffic. Almost half a million cars, trucks, and buses swarm onto city streets that are unable to handle half that number. Traffic jams are so horrendous it is usually faster to walk than to take a taxi. But the pedestrian's life is perilous, too. The polite Athenian motorist is one who beeps his horn before plunging through a red light.

Athens is crowded with modern apartment buildings and city traffic.

*The National Gardens (left) near Syntagma Square
and a rare, quiet moment in Omonoia Square (right)*

"Ban the private automobile," say some city planners. It might be the only practical solution because, aside from traffic nightmares, the horde of vehicles discharges tons of poison into the sky above the capital each year. On particularly windless days, an observer atop the Acropolis sees a ghastly white cloud blanketing the city with only a few high-rise rooftops poking their way through. Athens has become one of the most polluted capitals in Europe.

Some highlights of the modern city of Athens are Syntagma and Omonoia squares and several superb museums. Syntagma is an area of posh hotels, airline offices, and trendy restaurants. Lawyers and university students regularly argue politics at a park near the square. About a twenty-minute walk from Syntagma (be wary of the speeding cars) lies Omonoia Square, where eight major streets converge. This is a working class area and a fine

Besides ready-to-eat food, street vendors sell flowers and produce.

place to sample food sold by street vendors. These delights include spinach pie, feta cheese turnover, and a tempting assortment of barbecued meats.

Athens' National Archaeological Museum holds more masterpieces of ancient art than any other museum in the world. They range from tiny earrings to statues weighing several tons. One of the museum's most famous items is a gold death mask found at Mycenae and believed by Heinrich Schliemann to belong to King Agamemnon. Scholars devote months and even years to the study of exhibits in the museum.

The old face of Athens presents an altogether different picture from the modern city. Tumbling down from the north slope of the Acropolis is a delightful neighborhood called the Plaka. It is a confusing tangle of streets where most tourists get lost. But what a fascinating place to be lost in! During the day the narrow twisting

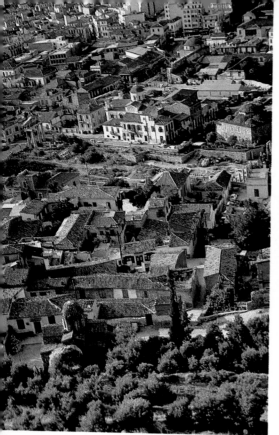

Left: A view of the Plaka from the Acropolis
Right: A shop near the Plaka

streets serve as a vast flea market, where vendors sell everything from genuine antiques and fine art work to assembly-line produced pottery. At night the Plaka is the city's entertainment headquarters, and bouzouki music and folk singing pour from its clubs and tavernas.

Near the Plaka are the remains of two agoras (marketplaces), one of which was built by the Romans. In Athens, where the works of antiquity are commonplace, the market built by the Romans is sometimes called the new agora. A feature of the Roman market is the Tower of Winds that once held an elaborate water clock. The Greek agora is almost as old as Athens itself. Tourists roaming through its rubble are thrilled by the thought that Socrates and his followers lived and taught on these grounds.

Certainly the highlight of any trip to Athens is a climb to the top of the Acropolis. The path one takes from the main parking lot

Scenes of Athens, counterclockwise
from top: the Agora with the
Acropolis in the background,
a grocery store, a residential
section, and a parakeet on a
windowsill in the old section

The Erechtheion (above) and the Propylaea (below),
two of the major buildings on the Acropolis

The Parthenon

follows the course of ancient processions. The hill's flat top
spreads about ten acres (four hectares) and holds the remains of
four major buildings—the Propylaea, the Temple of Athena Nike,
the Erechtheion, and the Parthenon. All were built during the
fifth century B.C., and when the wind whistles through their
pillars a visitor can almost hear the words of Pericles: "Future
ages will wonder at us as the present age wonders at us now."

The Acropolis is a fitting place to end the story of Greece. On its
top stand the monuments of a golden age; below spreads a city
where people confront the twentieth century. Despite nagging
unemployment and political uncertainty, Greeks believe their
future is bright. As the modern Greek poet Yannis Ritsos said,
"Don't weep for Greekhood. . . . It is rising again, brave and
fierce—piercing the beast with the spear of the sun."

MAP KEY

Lowercase letters refer to insert on bottom left

Agrínion	C3
Aidhipsoú	C4
Aitolikón	C3
AIYINA (AEGINA)	D4
Aíyina	D4
Aíyion	C4
Akharnaí	g11
AKRITIS	D6
Alepokhóri	g10
Alexandroúpolis	B5
Alistráti	B4
ALKIONIDHES	g9
Almirós	C4
Amaliás	D3
Amaroúsion	g11
Ámfissa	C4
AMORGÓS	D5
ANÁFI (ANAPHE)	D5
ANDÍKITHIRA	E4
ÁNDROS	D5
Andros	D5
Ano Theológos	B5
Ano Viánnos	E5
Anóyia	E5
Apíranthos	D5
Argalastí	C4
Árgos	D4
Árgos Orestikón	B3
Argostólion	C3
Árnissa	B3
Árta	C3
Asprópirgos	g11
Astakós	C3
ASTIPÁLAIA	D6
Atalándi	C4
Athens (Athinai)	D4, h11
Ayía	C4
Ayía Paraskeví	C6
Ayiássos	C6
Áyios	g11
Áyios Nikólaos	E5
Avlón	g11
CNOSSUS (KNOSSUS) (ruins)	E5
CRETE	E4, E5, E6
Dhekélia	g11
DHENOÚSA	D5
Dhidhimótikhon	B6
DHÍLOS (DELOS)	D5
Dhimítrios	g11
Dhimitsána	D4
Dhrítsa	g11
DÍA	E5
Domvraina	g9
Dráma	B5
Édhessa	B4
Ekhinos	C3
Elassón	C4
Elevsis (Eleusis)	g11
Eressós	C5
Erithraí	g11
EVSTRATIOS	C4, g10
Évvoia (Euboea)	C5
FANÓS	C4
Fársala	C2
Fili	C4
Filiatrá	g11
Flórina (Phlorina)	D3
Galaxidhion	B3
Gargaliánoi	C4
GÁVDHOS	D3
Gilifádha	E5
Grevená	h11
ÍDHRA (HYDRA)	C4
Ídhra	D5
Ierápetra	D5
Ierissós	E4
Igoumenítsa	D5
IKARÍA	D5
ILIODHRÓMIA	B4
Ioánnina	C3
íos	D6
Iráklion (Candia)	C4
Istiaía	C3
Itéa	D5
ITHÁKI (ITHACA)	C4
Itháki	E5
Kalámai	C4
Kalampáka	C4
Kalávrita	C3
KÁLIMNOS	C3
Kállithéa	D4
Kallithéa	D6
Kapandrítion	C3
Kardhítsa	C4
Kariaí	D6
Káristos	C3
Karlóvasi	C4
KÁRPATHOS	D6
Karpenísion	C4
KÁSOS	D6
Kastélli	D6
Kastoría	C3
Kástron	h11
Kateríni	C4
Katokhí	g11
Kavála	C3
KÉA	B5
Kéa	C5
KEFALLINÍA (CEPHALONIA)	D6
KÉRKIRA (CORFU)	E6
Kérkira	C3
KHALKÍ (CHALKE)	g11
Khalkís (Chalcis)	D5
Khaniá (Canea)	B6
KHIOS (CHIOS)	D5
Khios	g11
Khora Sfakíon	D4
Khrisoúpolis	g11
Kifisiá	E5
Kilkís	g9
Killíni	B5
Kimi	B4
Kiparissía	C2
KITHIRA (CYTHERA)	C2
Kíthira	D6
KÍTHNOS	g11
Komotiní	C4, g11
Kónitsa	C5, C6
Kórinthos (Corinth)	C6
Koropí	E5
KÓS (COS)	B5
Kós	g11
Kozáni	B4
Kranídhion	D3
Krokeaí	C5
Lamía	D3
Langadhás	D4
Lárisa	D5
Lávrion	B5
Leonídhion	B3
LÉROS	B4
LÉSVOS (LESBOS)	D4, h9
Levádhia	h11
LÉVITHOS	D6
LEVKÁS (LEUCAS)	D6
Levkás	B3
Lévktra	C3
Limní	C4
LIMNOS (LEMNOS)	B5
Líndhos	C5
Lípsos	D6
Litókhoron	E6
Loutrá	C3
Loutrákion	E6
Magoúla	E4
Mándra	B3
Marathón	C5
Markópoulon	B4
Megalópolis	C3
Mégara	C3
Mélambes	B5
Mesolóngion	D5
Messíni	D5
Methóni	C3
Métsovon	C3
MIKONOS	D5
Miléai	C4
MILOS	D5
Mitilíni (Mytilene)	C6
Moláoi	D4
Monemvasía	D4
MOUDHROS (MUDROS)	C5
Moúlki	g10
Náousa	B4
Návpaktos	C3
Návplion	D4
NÁXOS	C5
Náxos	D5
Néa Palátia	g11
Néa Psará (Erétria)	g11
Neápolis	D4
Neápolis	E5
Nestórion	B3
Nígrita	B4
NÍSIROS	D6
NORTHERN SPORADES	C5
Palaiokhóra	E4
Palaión Fáliron	h11
Paramithiá	C3
Párga	C3
PÁROS	D5
Páros	D5
PÁTMOS	D6
Pátrai (Patras)	C3
PAXÓI	C3
PÉLAGOS	C5
Perakhóra	g9
Pílos	D3
PIPERI	C5
Piraiévs (Piraeus)	D4, h11
Pírgos	D3
Plomárion	C6
Políkhnitos	C6
Políyiros	B4
Préveza	C3
Prosotsáni	B4
Psakhná	C4
PSARÁ	C5
Ptolemaís	B3
Réthimnon	E5
RÓDHOS (RHODES)	D6, D7
Ródhos	D7
SALAMÍS	h10, h11
Salamís	D4, g10
SÁMOS	D6
SAMOTHRÁKI (SAMOTHRACE)	B5
Sápai	B5
Sarande	C3
SARIA	E6
SÉRIFOS	D5
Sérifos	D5
Sérrai	B4
Sérvia	B4
Siátista	B3
Sidhirókastron	B4
SIFNOS	D5
Sikiá	B4
SIKINOS	D5
Sikionía	C4
SIMI	D6
SIRNAÍ	D6
SIROS	D5
Síros	D5
Sitía	E6
SKANTZOURA	C5
Skhimatárion	g11
SKIATHOS	C4
SKIROS (SCYROS)	C5
Skíros	C5
SKÓPELOS	C4
Sofádhes	C4
Souflíon	B6
Spárti (Sparta)	D4
Stílis	C4
STROFÁDHES	D3
THÁSOS	B5
Thásos	B5
Thérmon	C3
Thessaloníki (Salonika)	B4
THIRA	D5
Thívai (Thebes)	C4, g10
TÍLOS	D6
TÍNOS	D5
Tínos	D5
Tírnavos	C4
Topólia	g10
Trikkala (Tricca)	C3
Trípolis (Tripolitza)	D4
Vári	h11
Vathí	D6
Velestínon	C4
Véroia	B4
Villía	g10
Vólos	C4
Vónitsa	C3
Vouliagméni	h11
Xánthi	B5
Yiannitsá	B4
YIAROS	D5
YIOURA	C5
Yíthion	D4
Zagorá	C4
ZÁKINTHOS (ZANTE)	C3
Zákinthos	C3
Zevgolatió	D3

MINI-FACTS AT A GLANCE

GENERAL INFORMATION

Official Name: *Elliniki Dimokratia* (Hellenic Republic)

Capital: Athens

Official Language: Modern Greek

Government: Under the 1975 constitution, Greece has a parliamentary form of government. The two executive officers are the president and the prime minister. The prime minister sets government policy. Parliament consists of three hundred members who are elected to four-year terms. The Parliament is called the *Vouli*. One of its major functions is to prepare the budget.

Greece is divided into 53 prefectures (*nomoi*), each headed by a governor selected by the minister of the interior.

The voting age is eighteen; voting in parliamentary elections is required by law. Greek party politics has been dominated by volatile, shifting alliances among groups that are dominated by the personalities of their leaders.

National Anthem: *"Imnos pros tin Eleftherian"* ("The Hymn to Liberty")

Flag: A white cross in the top left-hand corner symbolizes the purity of the Greek Orthodox religion. Blue stripes represent the sea and the sky and white stripes stand for the Greek struggle for independence.

Money: The basic unit of currency is the drachma, with one hundred lepta, or cents, equaling one drachma. In the spring of 1987, the drachma was worth $.0082; 132 drachmas to the U.S. dollar.

Weights and Measures: Greece uses the metric system.

Population: 1981 census: 9,706,687; 66 percent urban, 34 percent rural. Estimated 1987 population, 10,042,000

Cities:

Athens	885,737
Metropolitan Athens	3,027,331
Thessaloníki	406,413
Metropolitan Thessaloníki	706,180
Piraeus	196,389

(Population figures based on 1981 census)

Religion: The official religion of Greece is Greek Orthodoxy. Though everyone has freedom of worship, Greek Orthodoxy is taught in the schools and the church is largely supported by government funds.

The church is governed under general state supervision by a holy synod, composed of twelve leading prelates, presided over by the archbishop of Athens.

Religion plays a major role in the national consciousness of the Greek people and has sustained them through many periods of foreign domination.

GEOGRAPHY

Highest Point: Mount Olympus, 9,570 ft. (2,917 m)

Lowest Point: sea level along the coasts

Coastline: 9,333 mi. (15,020 km), including islands

Mountains: The Pindus Mountains occupy the central part of the mainland; they are a southward continuation of the Dinaric Mountains of Yugoslavia and Albania. In the eastern part of the peninsula the mountains divide into small mountainous uplands that are separated by small depressions. The largest of these is the plain of Thessaly. North of this is Mount Olympus. Farther south a small mountain range extends from Mount Parnassos (8,061 ft.; 2,457 m) eastward to the coast.

Rivers: There are only a few rivers in Greece and they are short and swiftly flowing. The Arakhthos, Akheloos, Aliakmon, Pinios (Peneus), and Sperkhios rivers rise in the Pindus Mountains and flow to either the Ionian or the Aegean sea. Much of the Peloponnesus is drained by the Alfios (Alpheus) and Evrotas rivers. All these rivers drop steeply from the mountains down to narrow plains and then on to the sea. Most of these rivers dry up in the summer because of lack of rain.

Climate: The temperature in Athens can range from the sweltering heat of summer to cool winter days. Athens has little snowfall, though the mountains that surround the city often have enough snow for skiing. Northern Greece has a temperate climate. Temperatures range from 40° F. (4° C) in winter to above 75° F. (24° C) in summer. Rainfall occurs mostly from October to March with almost rainless summers.

Greatest Distances: Mainland, north to south—365 mi. (587 km)
East to west—345 mi. (555 km)

Area: 50,944 sq. mi. (131,944 km²)

NATURE

Trees: In the north and on the mountain flanks, central European types of vegetation prevail. In the central and southern regions and along mountain valleys, half of the land is scrub of various kinds; maquis, with oleander, bay, oak, olive, and juniper, is particularly prevalent in the Peloponnesus. Evergreens, shrubs, and herbaceous plants are found in the lowlands; pines, planes, and poplars along the rivers and coastal plains; oak, chestnut, and other deciduous trees in the north with Grecian firs at higher altitudes. The black-pine forests covering Mount Olympus are noteworthy.

Fish: There are good fishing grounds, but the fishing industry in Greece is strikingly underdeveloped.

Animals: The forested zones, especially in the north, contain European animals such as wildcat, martin, bear, deer, and, in smaller quantities, wolf, lynx, and wild boar. Animals of the Mediterranean region include jackal, wild goat, and porcupine.

Birds: Pelican, storks, and herons are plentiful, and many birds from farther north winter in sunny Greece.

EVERYDAY LIFE

Food: Lamb is the basis of the Greek diet. Fish and seafood from the Mediterranean are popular as well. Olive oil is used both for flavor and as a major ingredient in food preparation. *Dolmathes*, vine leaves filled with ground lamb and rice; *soupa augolemono*, lemon-flavored chicken soup; *moussaka*, eggplant and ground lamb, and *souvlakia*, meat roasted with onions and tomatoes on a skewer, are enjoyed not only by the people of Greece, but also by people all over the world who eat in Greek restaurants. Feta cheese and *ouzo*, an anise-flavored drink, are also important to the Greek table.

Housing: The average rural home consists of three or four rooms with earthen or wooden floors and whitewashed walls and shutters. Sanitation is underdeveloped. Even in the urban areas, housing is scarce and overcrowded and a major social concern.

Holidays:

January 1, Feast of St. Basil the Great
January 6, Feast of the Epiphany
January 30, Hellenic Letters Day, Festival of Schools
March 25, Independence Day and the Annunciation of the Virgin
Easter Sunday
April 23, Feast of St. George, Patron of Shepherds
May 1, Labor Day and Flower Festival
May 20, St. Constantine's Day
August 15, Dormition of the Virgin Mary, Festival of Countryside
October 26, St. Demetrios' Day, Festival of Demetria, Thessaloníki
October 28, Ochi Day commemorating Greek resistance against Fascism
December 6, St. Nicholas' Day, Patron of Sailors

December 12, Feast of St. Spyridon
December 25-26, Christmas Public Holidays

Culture: The physical remains of the culture of ancient and Byzantine/Medieval Greece are preserved in the fine network of museums both in Greece and in other countries (such as England). The deep religious traditions of the country are richly expressed in the Byzantine icons, mosaics, and frescoes that made the fourteenth century one of the most triumphant periods in Byzantine art.

The Academy of Athens strives to promote high standards in the arts, letters, and sciences. The most important libraries are the National Library, the Gennadeion, and the Library of the Chamber of Deputies, all located in Athens. The National Archaeological Museum in Athens contains works from Greek antiquity, and the Byzantine Museum has a rich collection of early Christian and Byzantine art. There are also museums at the archaeological sites at the Acropolis, Delphi, and Olympia.

Greek plays, particularly those of Aeschylus, Sophocles, and Euripides, are among the most important works in the world's literature. The summer months are known for a variety of international drama and music festivals. Greek music has an international following.

In modern literature, Greek poetry is considered among the best of the twentieth century. Poets of international renown include Constantine Cavafy, George Seferis, Odysseus Elytis, and Yannis Ritsos. Nikos Kazantzakis experimented with several forms of written expression.

Greek Alphabet:

A	α	alpha		N	ν	nu
B	β	beta		Ξ	ξ	xi
Γ	γ	gamma		O	o	omicron
Δ	δ	delta		Π	π	pi
E	ϵ	epsilon		P	ρ	rho
Z	ζ	zeta		Σ	σ	sigma
H	η	eta		T	τ	tau
Θ	θ	theta		Υ	υ	upsilon
I	ι	iota		Φ	ϕ	phi
K	κ	kappa		X	χ	chi
Λ	λ	lambda		Ψ	ψ	psi
M	μ	mu		Ω	ω	omega

Some Greek Words:

English	**Greek**	**American Pronunciation**
HELLO	χαίρετε	HEH-re-teh
GOOD-BYE	γειά σου} χαίρετε	YA-soo
PLEASE	παρακαλῶ	pah-rah-kah-LOH
THANK YOU	εὐχαριστῶ	eff-hah-rees-TOH
YOU'RE WELCOME	παρακαλῶ	pah-rah-kah-LOH
GOOD MORNING	καλημέρα	kah-lee-MEH-rah
YES	ταί }μάλιστα	NEH
NO	ὄξι	OH-hee
BOY	ἀγόρι	a-GORE-ee
GIRL	κορίθσι	co-REE-tsee

Sports and Recreation: The Greeks have a passion for soccer and basketball, too, is played all over the country at all age levels. In ancient Greece, the Olympic games were held in honor of the god Zeus. The first modern Olympic Games were held in 1896 in Athens.

Communication: Freedom of the press was guaranteed under the constitution of 1975. In the mid-seventies, total newspaper circulation was about one million. The largest daily newspaper is the *Acropolis* of Athens, which sells over 80,000 papers daily. The leading literary magazine is *New Estia* (New Hearth). Thousands of books, including translations of foreign works, are published annually.

The government owns the telephone and telegraph systems, as well as the radio and TV broadcasting systems.

Transportation: The railway network does not cover the entire country. One can go from Athens to Thessaloníki and from there on to Yugoslavia and Turkey. One cannot cross the Pindus spine, which runs vertically down the length of mainland Greece.

About one-third of the villages can be reached only by rough trails. Donkeys are still used. There are about 27,000 mi. (43,500 km) of roads and highways, and only about 5,000 mi. (8,000 km) have hard surfaces. There are about 1,600 mi. (2,570 km) of railroad track.

Greek shipping is of world importance, and as a result there is a strong emphasis on port development. Steamer hydrofoil service to the islands is in great demand.

Air transport is operated by the Government-owned Olympic Airways. Athens has a modern air terminal and regional facilities are being improved constantly.

Education: Education is the responsibility of the state, through the Ministry of National Education and Religion. An Education Act passed in 1964 introduced radical changes, making school attendance compulsory till the age of fifteen. It also made Demotic Greek (the colloquial language) the main language of instruction throughout the school system. Farm areas still have a shortage of educational institutions, and requirements for education are hardly ever enforced in those areas.

Junior secondary schools offer a three-year program. Advanced secondary schools also offer a three-year program. There are universities at Athens and at Thessaloníki. The University of Ioannina and the University of Patras are newer institutions.

Health: After World War II, efforts were made by the government to combat disease and establish modern health facilities and services. Malaria, once a serious scourge, has now been virtually eliminated, and standards of sanitation are largely improved. The World Health Organization also has worked with the government in reducing the number of deaths from infectious diseases. The Ministry of Social Services is responsible for health and medical care. There are large hospitals in Athens, Thessaloníki, and Patras. Social insurance schemes are coordinated by the Ministry of Social Services.

ECONOMY AND INDUSTRY

Principle Products:
Agriculture: olives, lemons, cotton, tobacco, vegetables, sheep, goats
Manufacturing: cigarettes, clothing, processed foods
Mining: lignite, bauxite, chromite

IMPORTANT DATES

3000-1500 B.C.—Minoans based on the island of Crete rule the eastern Mediterranean

1600-1100 B.C.—Mycenaean civilization in Peloponnese

c. 1150 B.C.—Mycenae leads the siege and sack of Troy

c. 850 B.C.—Homer composes the *Iliad* and the *Odyssey*

776 B.C.—First Olympic Games are held at Olympia

c. 780 B.C.—Greeks colonize southern Italy and Sicily (*Magna Graecia*)

c. 750 B.C.—Greek colonies in the Black Sea

546 B.C.—Persia conquers the Asiatic Greeks

509 B.C.—Democracy established in Athens by Cleisthenes

490 B.C.—Persians invade Greece; their king, Darius, is beaten by the Athenians at Marathón

480 B.C.—Battles among Greeks and Persians at Thermopylae and Salamis

478 B.C.—Athens founds the confederation of Delos to unify the Greeks; Golden Age of Pericles begins with writings of Herodotus, Aeschylus, and Sophocles

447 B.C.—Construction of the Parthenon

431 B.C.—Peloponnesian War breaks out between Athens and Sparta

404 B.C.—Athens surrenders, but culture flourishes under Socrates, Plato, Aristotle, Aristophanes, Thucydides, and Xenophon.

387 B.C.—Plato establishes his Academia, the oldest known university

362 B.C.—Thebes defeats Athens and Sparta

358 B.C.—Philip of Macedonia starts his conquests

336 B.C.—Philip is murdered; Alexander the Great elected general of the Greeks

327 B.C.—Conquest of the Persian Empire by Alexander; fusion among Greeks and Persians

323 B.C.—Alexander dies; spread of Greek language and culture among all civilized peoples

300 B.C.—Hellenistic Age starts; Colossus of Rhodes erected

280 B.C.—Ptolemy, king of Egypt, translates Old Testament into Greek

146 B.C.—Corinth invaded; Greece becomes a Roman province; Athens is the leading university of the empire and Greek culture becomes universal

A.D. 331—Emperor Constantine the Great builds Constantinople; Roman Empire divides into east and west; Greece becomes a province of Byzantium, or Eastern Roman Empire, or Constantinople

379—Christianity becomes official religion of Byzantine Empire

527—Justinian the Great becomes emperor of Byzantium and lawgiver and wins back Italy, Spain, and North Africa; great age of the Byzantine Empire follows

532-537—Justinian builds Hagia Sophia, the biggest Greek Orthodox church

726—The Iconoclastic conflict, a crisis among Greek Orthodoxy in the definition of worship and church policy

843—End of Iconoclastic conflict, restoring the icons in church; triumph of Orthodoxy

857—Photius, an intellectual, becomes the religious leader, or patriarch, of the Orthodox church; Greek Orthodox art and culture at its best

1054—Separation (schism) between Western (Catholic) and Eastern (Orthodox) Christianity

1204—Crusaders invade Greece; Constantinople is sacked

1261—Revival of the Byzantine Empire

1453—Ottoman Empire gains Constantinople, the Byzantine capital; the last Greek Byzantine Emperor, Constantine Palaiologos, dies in combat

1821-29—Greek War of Independence; Ottoman Turks are defeated; Greece is formed

1827—Recognition of Greek independence by France, Great Britain, and Russia; Joannes Capodistria becomes first governor

1832—Otto I becomes Greece's first king

1844—Greece becomes a constitutional monarchy

1864—King George I establishes a more democratic constitution

1890-1925—Greek mass immigration to the United States

1909-10—Major reforms result from a military revolt

1912-13—Greece gains land in the Balkan wars

1917-18—Greece helps defeat Germany and her allies in World War I

1922—Greek forces are crushed by the Turks; Asia Minor Greeks are uprooted, some move to Greece as refugees or to the U.S.A. as immigrants

1924—Greece becomes a republic

1935—Constitutional monarchy is restored

1936—Dictatorship of Joannes Metaxas

1941-44—Germans and their allies occupy Greece during World War II

1946-49—Greek civil war; Communist-led rebels are defeated on August 30, 1949

1948—Prose writer Nikos Kazantzakis publishes his renowned novel, *Zorba the Greek*

1963—Poet George Seferis honored, the first Greek to receive the Nobel Prize

1967—Establishment of military dictatorship; King Constantine II leaves Greece

1973—Reestablishment of Greek republic, Parliamentary democracy replaces dictatorship.

1974—Civilian government formed; Parliamentary elections held; Turkish troops occupy northern Cyprus, Greek population flees to south

1981—Greece joins European Economic Community

IMPORTANT PEOPLE

Alexander the Great (356-323 B.C.), gained ascendancy over all of Greece, most of the Mediterranean, and the Persian Empire

Anaxagoras (c. 500-c. 428 B.C.), philosopher and scientist

Aristophanes (c. 448-c. 380 B.C.), Athenian playwright; one of the greatest comedians and dramatists of all time

Aristotle (384-322 B.C.), philosopher and teacher

Maria Callas (1923-77), Greek-American operatic soprano

Joannes Capodistria (1767-1831), statesman, first governor of Modern Greece

Cimon (c. 507-c. 449 B.C.), Athenian statesman and general

Constantine the Great (306-337), son of Greek Lady Helen, founded Constantinople, the capital city of the Byzantine Empire

Constantine I (1868-1923), king from 1913-17 and 1920-22

Demosthenes (384-322 B.C.), Athenian orator and statesman

Odysseus Elytis, (1911-   ), poet; winner of the Nobel Prize for Literature in 1979

Euclid (?-c. 300 B.C.), geometer and founder of modern geometry

Euripides (c. 484-406 B.C.), playwright and dramatist

George Gemistos-Plethon (1355-1452), philosopher, teacher, and classicist

121

George I (1845-1913), king from 1863-1913

George II (1890-47), King from 1922-23 and 1935-47

Germanos (1771-1826), patriot, archbishop of Patras

Petros Haris (1905-   ), writer, editor of leading journal *Nea Estia*

George Hatzidakis (1846-1923), linguist and professor

Manos Hatzidakis (1924-   ), musician and composer

Herodotus (fifth century B.C.), traveler and historian, known as "Father of History"

Hippocrates (460?-?377 B.C.), physician

Homer (c. 850-c. 775 B.C.), author of the *Iliad* and the *Odyssey*, the oldest written poems of Greece and Western civilization

Andreas Kalvos (1792-1869), poet whose odes were inspired by the Greek classics

Panagiotis Kanellopoulos (1902-1986), statesman and writer

Constantine Karamanlis (1907-   ), premier and leading political figure of contemporary Greece

Andreas Karkavitsas, (1860-1922), medical doctor and writer of short stories and novels

Nikos Kazantzakis (1883-1957), novelist, essayist, poet, and translator; author of *Zorba the Greek*

Theodoros Kolokotronis (1770-1843), leader in war for independence

Fotis Kontoglou (1896-1965), writer and painter of Byzantine icons

Adamandios Korais (1748-1833), scholar and patriot, who lived in Paris, France

Solon Kydoniatis (1906-   ), architect, academician

Spyridon Lambros (1847-1924), historian and statesman

Joannes Makrygiannis (1797-1864), patriot, general, and writer, although he was an illiterate

Spyridon Marinatos (1900-74), archaeologist and scholar

Nestor Matsas (1934-   ), artist, journalist, documentary director

Melina Mercouri (1926-   ), actress and political activist

Joannes Metaxas (1871-1941), general and politician; dictator from 1936-40

Alexis Minotis (1904-   ), actor and theater performer

Dimitri Mitropoulos (1896-1960), orchestral conductor of international stature

Myron (c. 480-440 B.C.), sculptor

Aristotle Onassis (1900-75), businessman and shipowner

Kostis Palamas (1859-1943), poet

Alexandros Papadiamadis (1851-1911), writer of short stories about village life

Gregory Papaflessas (1786-1825), statesman, patriot, and clergyman

Andreas Papandreou (1919-   ), prime minister in 1981, 1985

George Papandreou (1887-1968), prime minister in 1944, 1964

Katina Paxinou (1902-65), actress

Pericles (c. 495-429 B.C.), Athenian statesman, the model for democratic leader

Pheidippides (?-490 B.C.), Athenian long-distance runner dispatched to Sparta to seek aid before the Battle of Marathón

Phidias (fifth century B.C.), the greatest ancient Greek sculptor; designed the sculptures on the Parthenon

Photius (820-92), religious leader, intellectual, and writer

Plato (c. 428-348 or 347 B.C.), philosopher and writer

Plutarch (c. 46-after 119 A.D.), historian and biographer

Nicholaos Politis (1841-1924), professor and folklorist

Polyclitus (fifth century B.C.), sculptor

Protagoras (c. 485-410 B.C.), philosopher

Yiannis Psycharis (1852-1928), linguist, pro-Demotic language, and professor at Sorbonne in Paris, France

Yannis Ritsos (1909-   ), poet

George Seferis (1900-71), poet and diplomat; winner of Nobel Prize for Literature in 1963

Angelos Sikeliknos (1886-1951), poet, intellectual, and founder of the Delphic Games (1927)

Socrates (c. 470-399 B.C.), philosopher and teacher

Dionysios Solomos (1798-1859), considered the national poet of Greece

Solon (c. 630-c. 560 B.C.), Athenian lawgiver and statesman

Sophocles (c. 490-c. 406 B.C.), playwright and dramatist

Alexandros Soutsos (1803-63), poet influenced by European romanticism

Mikis Theodorakis (1925-   ), composer and political activist

Domenikos Theotokopoulos (1548?-1614), known as El Greco, became the foremost painter of the Castilian school in Spain

Thucydides (c. 460-c. 400 B.C.), historian

Spyridon Trikoupis (1790-1868), statesman and historian

Constantine Tsatsos (1899-   ), statesman and writer

Aristotelis Valaoritis (1824-79), poet and politician

Eleutherios Venizelos (1864-1936), statesman and diplomat

Dimitrios Ypsilanti (1785-1828), patriot and general; Ypsilanti, Michigan, was named after him in 1823

INDEX

Page numbers that appear in boldface type indicate illustrations.

About the Author

R. Conrad Stein was born in Chicago and was graduated from the University of Illinois with a degree in history. He now lives in Chicago with his wife, who is also an author of books for young readers, and their daughter, Janna. Mr. Stein has written many other books, articles, and short stories for young people.

To prepare for writing this book Mr. Stein traveled to Greece and toured the cities, farm villages, and ancient sites. He spoke to all classes of Greek people, from lawyers to shepherds. Greece's enchanting countryside and people thrilled the author and he longs to return to this friendly land. Mr. Stein wishes especially to thank Pat and Nick Yassoglou for inviting him to their home in the hills above Athens to enjoy a lovely *Kathari Deftera* (Clean Monday) party.